War[illegible]ealers

SPECIAL FORCES

AIRBORNE

Warrior Healers

The Untold Story of the Special Forces Medic

Book I:
The Beginning

Leonard D. Blessing Jr.

iUniverse, Inc.
New York Lincoln Shanghai

Warrior Healers
The Untold Story of the Special Forces Medic

iUniverse books may be ordered through booksellers or by contacting:

iUniverse
2021 Pine Lake Road, Suite 100
Lincoln, NE 68512
www.iuniverse.com
1-800-Authors (1-800-288-4677)

ISBN-13: 978-0-595-40256-4 (pbk)
ISBN-13: 978-0-595-84631-3 (ebk)
ISBN-10: 0-595-40256-9 (pbk)
ISBN-10: 0-595-84631-9 (ebk)

Printed in the United States of America

Dedicated to all past, present and future Special Forces medics.
In memory of Alan B. Maggio and Carey 'Drum' Drumheller.

Carey "Drum" Drumheller (L) and Colonel Aaron Bank, Bad Tolz, Bavaria 1954. (Provided by Carey Drumheller)

Sergeant First Class Alan B. Maggio (L) carrying M-2 carbine and Sergeant First Class John Edmunds (Weapons Sergeant). Laos, 1962. (Provided by Alan B. Maggio)

Special Forces Aidman's Pledge

As a Special Forces Aidman of the United States Army, I pledge my honor and my conscience to the service of my country and the art of medicine.

I recognize the responsibility, which may be placed upon me for the health, and even lives, of others.

I confess the limitation of my skill and knowledge in the caring for the sick and injured.

I promise to follow the maxim "Primum non nocere" ("First, thou shalt do no harm"), and to seek the assistance of more competent medical authority whenever it is available.

Those confidences, which come to me in my attendance on the sick, I will treat as secret.

I recognize my responsibility to impart to others who seek the service of medicine such knowledge of its art and practice as I possess, and I resolve to continue to improve my capability to this purpose.

As an American soldier, I have determined ultimately to place above all considerations of self, the mission of my team and the cause of my nation.

Contents

Appendices

List of Illustrations

PREFACE

The objective of this series of books is to document and relay the incredible story of the Special Forces Medic. It is not intended to separate or elevate them above any of the other specialties that comprise a Special Forces Team. The team is first and foremost the most important aspect of Special Forces. Each individual specialty supports and compliments the other.

A proud sense of history and tradition has developed among the United States Army Special Forces in its short lifetime of 50 years. During this time there has been much written about their exploits around the world, mostly, concentrating around the Vietnam War. Vietnam gave rise and attention to the men who wear the Green Beret. There is an aura and mystique that has surrounded this group since its birth as the "bastard child" of the OSS (Office of Strategic Services).

Unfortunately there is a myth that exists, in spite of the many accurate and truthful accountings, of a ruthless, out of control, brawling malcontent and a 'blood thirsty killer'. There exists a myriad of derogatory names and ridiculous stereotypes that describe the men of Special Forces that should be put to rest. Special Forces soldiers have and continue to conduct themselves with the highest level of professionalism, representing what the United States embodies.

This first book details the developmental stages of this unique soldier. I must admit that I had absolutely no idea what I was embarking upon. Never could I have imagined the intricacy and scope the project would encompass. Originally, the concept was to relay the story of Vietnam War era Special Forces medics. Once the process of research and documentation of the achievements and experiences began, it became apparent that to focus on that period alone would be a major injustice to the medical developments contributed by medics throughout the history of Special Forces. The early years prior to involvement in Vietnam brimmed with evolutionary triumph in the face of many obstacles and deterrents. These events contributed and impacted the medics that served in Vietnam dramatically. Their experiences are still deeply embedded in the training process and operational use today.

My preconceived definitions of the word 'medic' were quickly obliterated once the scope of the Special Forces medics' training and abilities began to surface. Usually, upon hearing the word, it is natural to think of the traditional combat medic in an infantry line unit. This is not a slander toward the brave men that performed and continue to perform heroically in that capacity. In fact, many of the early volunteers were medics with combat experience during World War II and Korea as traditional regular army medics. The Special Forces medic is quick to profess his admiration and respect for his fellow healers.

Ironically, the process of writing this story developed through patient trial and error, much like the medical specialist did, evolving and changing with each facet uncovered. The ever-expanding project led to the realization that the volumes of information could not possibly be contained within the cover of one book. Subsequent books will document, through each decade, the refinement and evolution of the Special Forces Medical Sergeant. Every medic, past and present, has contributed to the story and the development of the medical aidman specialty.

Several years of conducting surveys', phone calls, personal meetings, letters and email correspondence brought everything together, medic and non-medic alike contributing to the effort. They have shared emotional memories of their experiences, both good and bad. Most often they caused laughter hard enough to hurt and at times somber enough to bring a lump to your throat. Getting the men to talk about themselves was, without a doubt, the most difficult aspect of research. But, as time passed and friendships formed, they shared their thoughts and feelings unabashedly.

Finally the story of the Special Forces medic is being told, in their words. This is a very important aspect of the project. *Their words* are used extensively to tell the story. There is no need to embellish or portray this story in any other manner except the truth. It is a story of life and death, humor, joy, sadness, compassion and bravery.

The memories obtained through this effort are something that will always be very special to me, and it has been a pleasure to begin documenting their efforts and sacrifices. Finally, they can be recognized for the unselfish and positive actions carried out with compassion and professionalism. I have found during the course of research the most helpful, compassionate and considerate human beings I have ever had the privilege of meeting and I thank you all for being patient, nurturing and most of all, my friends. I am humbled you chose me to tell your story.

It is with great pride and pleasure; I present the story of the United States Army Special Forces Medical Sergeant.

ACKNOWLEDGEMENTS

I am hesitant to attempt naming everyone involved with bringing this first book to completion for fear of omitting anyone. Honestly, another book could be written thanking all the individuals and groups that took an active part assisting the research and development of this project. Everyone shares equal credit and deserves my deepest thanks, without their participation this would not have been possible.

Omission of impassioned thanks to Lieutenant Colonel Louis Dorogi (USA Ret.) would be tantamount to a crime. From August 1975 to February 1978 Lou was assigned to the Army Medical Department (AMEDD) History Unit, much of his time was spent collecting information and interviewing participants for a project entitled *History of Special Forces AMEDD Operations in Vietnam.* Lou unselfishly shared his unpublished personal papers, files, photos and memories with me and asked for nothing in return. His efforts and dedication to the story of the medical activities of the Special Forces deserves to be recognized. Without his tireless assistance, support, expertise, and his extensive research these books would have taken an unknown number of years to complete.

I also extend thanks to Colonel Warner D. "Rocky" Farr, M.D. Command Surgeon, USSOCOM (United States Special Operation Command). Rocky, a Vietnam era Special Forces medic joined the effort to tell this story from the very beginning. His interest and support have provided invaluable assistance and brought further legitimacy to the project. His office, no matter how inundated with business matters, never failed to assist me. I would also like to thank Master Sergeant Russell Justice, long time NCOIC in Colonel Farr's office while stationed at Fort Bragg. I hope to someday be in a position to repay MSG Justice for his never ending dedication and assistance.

Also deserving of endless appreciation for assistance and support during research is Ms. Cynthia Hayden, Chief of the Archives Division for the Department of Education of the John F. Kennedy Special Warfare Center and School (JFKSWC). Cyn and her staff opened their office at the U.S. Army Special Operations Forces Archives (ARSOF), shared their expertise and tolerated incessant questions.

Mr. Charles Berg deserves credit for assisting with opening many doors to the Special Forces community by providing a letter of support requesting all Special Forces Association Chapter members lend their support in the effort when the project began in April 2000. Without it, the process of research would have been more difficult to initiate. I also wish to extend my gratitude to Mr. Jimmy Dean, his support at the national level of the Special Forces Association also had a tremendous impact upon the success of the project.

Finally, my deepest appreciation to the following for their time, energy and effort to help bring this first book to fruition. Chalmers Archer, Fred Baier, Paul Campbell, Don Dougan, Carey Drumheller, Al Gunn, Leigh Hotujec, Colonel Kevin Keenen, Robert Leonpacher, Alan Maggio, Roxanne Merritt, Ned Miller, Vladimir Mohar, Edward Montgomery, Earle Peckham, Herbert Schandler and Stephen Sherman.

INTRODUCTION

> "The medical specialist is responsible for the health of the detachment and the guerilla force; the medical training of guerilla personnel; and when the situation permits he can assist in winning the support of the local populace to the cause of the guerilla force by administering first aid to the civilians in the area. He must be proficient in all aspects of first aid to include minor surgery, emergency dental care, and sanitation, establishment of guerilla hospitals, evacuation procedures and medical supply and re-supply procedures. The Medical Specialist is assisted in the performance of his duties by the Assistant Medical Specialist. This man must have the same skills as the Medical Specialist. When the detachment is split he assumes the responsibility for medical activities for the portion of the detachment which he is attached."[1]

The Special Forces medic is unique among a group of unique individuals. He embodies what the American soldier represents. He is a highly trained professional soldier who is compassionate and caring to those he is asked to help. 'Doc', is an expression of respect and trust by his team and the people he treats. 'Doc', spoken in any language, conveys the immense capabilities and responsibilities of the medic, and the love that is felt for him by all those with whom he comes into contact. There is no greater love than that which exists between the men of the Special Forces and their 'Doc'. His role with the team is that of a warrior first and healer second. This aspect of the medic can not be stressed enough; it is what makes him so unique. Each soldier, be it a team member or a guerilla fighter, knows the medic will come to his aid during the chaos of combat and its aftermath, to provide physical and mental healing. "The story of the Special Forces medic is one of deep commitment and passion that displays a little known side of war. You can be true to your mission and country, but also display a human side to your fellow man."[2] A SF medic requires a special skill set coupled with the ability to perform in a non-traditional setting, for there is no such beast for Special Forces. SF medics deployed to await the return of Apollo space mission astronauts who may require medical attention upon their return to earth. They provided medical aid to the inhabitants of small countries suffering from floods and other natural disasters and the ensuing chaos of disease outbreak. They set up medical aid stations here in the United States to provide much needed care during national disasters. The scenarios under which medics have plied their skills are nearly infinite.

The Special Forces medics' accomplishments through perseverance, heroism and dedication are a story few people know. Their training and skills have developed and advanced to meet the needs of the United States Army Special Forces (Airborne) mission. The medical training is rigorous, demanding and extensive. The formalized training cycle has evolved to become distinguished as the only form of Army medical training for enlisted personnel not under the full command of Ft. Sam Houston's, Brooke Army Medical Center. Of the five basic Special Forces specialties, it is the most lengthy and concentrated training cycle. The time invested to train a medic lasts over one year.[3] The training cycles are segmented into separate phases witnessing substantial attrition rates throughout the process. The training portion of medical training culminates with students facing a pass/fail oral (board) examination.

The Special Forces medic is trained to perform far more than emergency first aid techniques on the battlefield and there is always one rule in practice: 'Do No Harm'. This means the medic is trained in advanced medical procedures, but he is always to perform within his boundaries. "Perhaps the most important of all was the requirement for the medical enlisted man to understand his limitation—the Special Forces medical specialist is not a doctor and always reminded that he must never assume that he is one. His training, therefore, is thorough and varied. He is trained to act and think as a physician and trained with the aim in mind that under adverse conditions and hundreds of miles behind enemy lines,…he almost certainly will have to perform certain operations such as amputations, debridements, and tracheotomies, treat major illnesses, and perhaps even deliver babies."[4] "His first commandment is that he should understand, accept and practice the Special Forces Aidman's Medical Creed[5], which described the limits of his right to perform medical services. It is his Hippocratic Oath."[6] Upon graduation from training, the medic is prepared to participate in unconventional warfare, in locations ranging from snow covered mountains in South Asia to the steaming jungles of South America. In addition to his combat arms role, he provides medical care for the team, the indigenous troops they are training, and their dependents. His training has prepared him to be the only source of medical care, operating far from support with limited communications to the outside world.

The nature of unconventional warfare (UW) requires him to be prepared for any situation that may require limited general surgery—such as the debridement and suturing of wounds, extracting bullets and shrapnel, prescribing and dispensing medication, setting broken bones, identifying diseases and implementing strategies to eliminate and prevent them, dentistry, delivering babies, developing sanitation practices, veterinary services and much more. The demands placed upon the medic to perform in these surroundings are incomprehensible to most. They can face situations that many emergency room medical professionals will ever be faced with in a lifetime of practice.

The medics' mission is not limited to warfare. The extensive training dedicates a tremendous amount of time to preventive measures to avoid, or at least minimize, injury, sickness and disease. All of this training also emphasizes the role of the medic as an educator. This is an integral part of the Special Forces mission—teaching those that they are assisting how to continue these programs after the team leaves. This concept is referred to as 'force multiplier'. A twelve man detachment is capable of training hundreds of men.

To fully appreciate the role, responsibilities and accomplishments of the Special Forces medic, a basic understanding is needed of the Special Forces Group organization[7] and its mission in unconventional warfare doctrine. The one constant of the Special Forces original mission was to develop, organize, equip and direct indigenous forces in the conduct of guerilla warfare. Often, the Special Forces team was the first and only contact with Americans that host country inhabitants experienced. In a sense, the Special Forces are ambassadors of our nation's foreign policy. Special Forces members also undergo intensive area specific training for eventual deployment in the Group's assigned region of operations. The Special Forces Group has an inherent flexibility to tailor teams for a rapid response to any assigned mission. Missions may encompass planning and conducting unconventional warfare, stability operations or direct action peculiar to Special Forces. The 'A' Detachment is the basic component of Special Forces operations. The standard composition of a Special Forces Operational Detachment (SFOD) is: a Commanding Officer (CO), Executive Officer (XO) and 10 non-commissioned officers extensively trained in each of the following specialties; Intelligence and Operations (2), Heavy Weapons (1), Light Weapons (1), Communications (2), Engineer/Demolitions (2) and Medicine (2). They teach and lead indigenous peoples in the art of guerilla warfare, operating as a self contained unit with virtually no outside support.

The terminology for structural organization has changed over the years, but for simplification we will examine the basic organization during the 1960's.[8] There were four or more 'A' Detachments, also known as 'A' Teams, under the operational control of a 'B' Detachment, which in turn were under the control of a 'C' Detachment in a Special Forces Company. Each 'A' Team had two medics, a junior and senior non-commissioned officer (NCO). Each 'B' Team had a Chief Medical NCO who is assisted by a preventive medicine specialist. The 'B' Detachment medical role could vary widely, but was by and large the administrative arm that facilitated getting the necessary support out to the individual 'A' Teams. The 'B' Team's medical personnel monitored medical problems, consolidated reports from the 'A' Teams and provided preventive medicine support as needed. In some cases, especially in support of Special Operations, there was a small hospital unit for treating heavy casualties. Generally speaking, the 'A' and 'B' Detachments were not staffed by a medical officer, leaving the senior medic of the detachment responsible for the setup and operation of the medical facilities, including minor surgery and laboratory practices. 'C' Team medical personnel were provided through the Medical Platoon, which was under the operational control of the Group Surgeon. It is at this level that a broad range of medical treatment and preventive medicine policies of the Group were carried out, including clinical follow up and hospitalization. There were 16 AMEDD (Army Medical Department) officers and 36 NCO's, who operated a dispensary for the treatment of refugees and recovering indigenous personnel. The 'C' Team also provided a manpower replacement pool for the 'A' and 'B' Teams. The medical platoon consisted of four primary teams:

1. Medical Platoon HQ: Administrative, medical training, supply and records support.
2. Medical Team: Provide dental, pharmaceutical and laboratory services.
3. Preventive Medicine Team: Preventive medicine, field sanitation, food procurement and preservation, medical intelligence and veterinary programs.
4. Medical Operations Team: Four separate six man teams that are deployed with either the 'A' or 'C' detachment for medical planning and supervision.[9]

An 'A' Detachment medic operates in an unconventional warfare environment located in a remote and possibly hostile territory for extended periods of time with limited communications capability. Operating without direct supervision from a military physician places tremendous responsibility on the detachment medic. His immediate supervisor is a combat arms officer since the medics' first priority is being a soldier. The medic is answerable for the medical training and support of a guerilla force of up to 1,500 personnel. He is the detachment commanders' principal medical advisor and his duties cover a wide range. These include medical civic action, public health, preventive medicine, medical supply and the planning and construction of medical facilities. The medics' role is of paramount importance to the success of the mission. He is responsible for the medical care of his team; he also renders medical assistance to indigenous people they assist and train. In most cases, he is the closest thing to a doctor the people may ever encounter. The medic will often have to gain the peoples trust by dealing with their superstitions and convincing the local healers that his medicine used in conjunction with local procedures, is more effective.

The unconventional warfare environment places a greater emphasis for the need of well-qualified enlisted medical personnel who are capable of operating independently. In a conventional warfare setting, serious medical problems are evacuated to a higher level of medical care such as, battalion aid stations, hospital ships and rear area hospital facilities equipped with modern equipment and staffed with doctors and nurses. The Special Forces medic is often required to improvise equipment and facilities and assume the roles of nursing and doctoring because medical evacuation often can not be expected in unconventional warfare. These unconventional warfare conditions emphasized the need for a physician oriented training program for the enlisted medic.

Now, with this foundation in place, it becomes much clearer why the SF medic receives such extensive training to perform his duty within the unit. The Special Forces medic is expected to assume the role, if need be, of an infantry leader, leading indigenous troops during military operations. They can perform area studies to identify and document disease endemic of the host countries, providing valuable medical intelligence for troops operating in those regions. They are trained to observe and record the smallest of details including exposure to environmental surroundings such as swamps, rivers, plant growth and the types of food ingested and the manner in which this food is prepared. To the medic, the most important aspect of the mission is the people; their customs, beliefs, housing, domestic animals, and their diets. This information, collected by the medic, helps answer important medical questions.

SF medics must use innovative thinking to adapt to any situation and utilize resources available to accomplish their mission. Extensive testing and training determine whether they possess the physical and mental toughness to succeed and survive under harsh environments and stressful situations. Every medic attests that the training is by far the most academically challenging instruction they had ever experienced. They endure the longest and toughest mental challenge the Army has to offer for any MOS (military occupational skill). The academic regimen, which produces a high attrition rate, must be mastered in addition to the physically tough Special Forces core training that produces the best trained soldier in the U.S. Army. The lyrics from the popular song 'The Ballad of the Green Beret', written by Sgt. Barry Sadler (May 1964 Medical Specialist graduate)—illustrate the difficulty of becoming a member of Special Forces:

"These are men, America's best,
One hundred men we'll test today,
But only three win the Green Beret."[10]

The length of the medical training phases has changed over the course of the past fifty years with the constant adaptations for lessons learned in the field. The medics have been called upon to meet many challenges all over the world, as well as at home. As those that went before them, active duty medics will set the example for others to follow. All of their contributions are rooted in one common factor; they believe their training and accomplishments have directly impacted all of their endeavors. Some served and retired from a full Special Forces career in medical and non-medical capacities. For example, a full medical military career was not limited to Special Forces. A number of them became medical instructors, physician assistants and surgeons in the Armed Forces. Others took their skills to the civilian sector, again to become physician assistants, doctors, emergency medical technicians, lab specialists, and medical specialists for prisons and oil drilling rigs. Some never followed a medical career after their service and went on to become engineers, teachers, government officials, secret service agents, small business owners, advertising, financial, operations executives and even cowboys. Whichever path they chose they all agree their training and experiences as a Special Forces medic had a positive impact upon their lives, and that of many others.

PROLOGUE

20 June 2002, Fort Bragg North Carolina

A charter bus rolled to a slow stop in front of the Joint Special Operations Medical Training Center (JSOMTC). The men aboard grew quiet as the realization weighed heavy that the moment has finally arrived—they have come home.

The bus ride was filled with an almost giddy anticipation as multiple conversations intermixed. Only snippets could be heard from each. Individual recollections combined to form one story. All of the passengers had survived the rigorous Special Forces Medical Training program. Some were former class mates; others had made the journey alone. This one accomplishment in their lives had bound them all together as brothers. A father and son team the son following in his fathers' footsteps.[11] This group of individuals collectively forms a unique and special bond that transcends the boundaries of time, making them one. Many had not been back to Ft. Bragg for almost 40 years. Most had not seen each other since receiving orders after completing their training, but here, it was as if it was just yesterday. Time had made bellies grow a little bigger, hair had thinned and turned gray but the youthful faces from long ago snapshots glowed with anticipation and the remembrance of distant memories. As the bus neared its destination a youthful exuberance and excitement filled the air with electricity. Eyes were wide and bright, but filled with memories of another lifetime. Many of the memories were filled with happiness and laughter, but there was a silent undertone of sorrow that was unmistakable—it was the memory of the many that had made the ultimate sacrifice. The toughest task they had ever undertaken had begun as a great adventure filled with a youthful proud arrogance.

A welcoming party befitting returning hero's greeted the bus. The visitors represented a proud tradition that had started fifty years ago, exactly to the day. The United States Army Special Forces (Airborne) came into existence on Smoke Bomb Hill, Fort Bragg, North Carolina. The men were greeted with 'Hellos', handshakes and smiles as they descended the steps of the bus. Leading the welcoming committee was Colonel Warner 'Rocky' Farr, United States Special Operations Command Surgeon and former Vietnam era Special Forces medic; Colonel Kevin Keenen, JSOMTC Command Surgeon; Command Sergeant Major Jay Lovelace, Special Forces Training Group senior non-commissioned officer; and several other senior enlisted training cadre. The past was meeting the present.

The term 'former' is inappropriate because once someone has earned the right to wear the Green Beret; he is forever a member of the Special Forces family. The returning medics, who never considered their time here as momentous or historical, were now faced with their legacy. The groups (another tour had taken place earlier in the day) that visited the facility that day were represented by nearly every generation of medics from 1952 to 2002. The immensity of the facility struck them immediately. The 'old' Medical Lab could have fit into the new building several times over. A short distance away, all that stands of the former 'Lab', is a rusting fence topped with barbed wire. Thousands of commuters pass it every day-unnoticed. It was once a forbidden area and serves as a silent reminder to a storied past. The group was ushered into a conference room, all eyes filled with wonderment inside the state of the art facility. The tour began with a briefing consisting of some background information on the Program of Instruction (POI) and what today's medics are encountering, especially in Afghanistan, where today's warrior/healers are participating in the war against terror.[12] Throughout the presentation, there was a hushed astonishment as the advances in training and technology were discussed. The immense pride and even envy felt by the 'old' medics filled the room.

Current technological advances in training are incredible, but the same basic dedication is evident in modern era SF medics. It is the desire to be the best, so that he, the 'Doc', will be there to care for them under any circumstances and administer medical aid. However, what is it that makes the SF medic such an interesting and diverse individual? He is, above all else, a warrior. He can, and does, function as a combatant, shouldering that responsibility alongside his team members, to inflict damage against the enemy. The medical training is designed to produce an individual who is capable of operating independently in the harshest of conditions with very little or no support/supervision from medical professionals. Colonel Keenen provided his perspective on how, in an extraordinarily short period of time, these men are trained to handle this immense responsibility. He compared the Special Forces medical training with civilian medical training by saying; "Physician training in the United States is two years of classroom and two years of clinical. Physician Assistant (PA) training is one year of classroom and one year of clinical. Special Forces Medical Sergeant training is six months of classroom and six months of clinical." The fast paced training schedule thins out the ranks very quickly. The brutal regimen is evident through Colonel Keenen's remarks to each incoming class of 100 or so students. "Gentlemen, look to your left and your right—two of you will not be here at the end of this course."

After completion of the briefing, the group was led throughout the facility's classrooms and laboratories. A shocked disbelief was almost always present on the faces of the 'old' warriors. The classrooms were plentiful and the equipment was the latest and best available. One element that had not changed over time was the instructors. The training cadre was comprised of confident and experienced professionals. This constant is the backbone of the training program. Only experienced peers can possibly appreciate the skills and abilities that will one day be required of the medics passing though the training facility. The classroom facilities are mesmerizing. In the physiology labs, students study the internal organs, vessels, muscles, bones and tissues of the human body by dissecting cadavers provided by the School of Medicine at the University of North Carolina. Here, in state of the art operating rooms they can familiarize themselves with intricate workings of the human body. They are putting the tax payers' money to full use with the ten 'Human Patient Simulators.' These computerized 'patients' are capable of being programmed with symptoms and wounds that range from the common cold to extensive head injuries and chest wounds. These wonders of science and technology come at a cost of $200,000 each, a small investment when the amount of 'real time' training accomplished is considered.

The next stop on the tour was the mass trauma unit. It is here that the students function as an emergency medical team under the stress and chaos of a mass casualty situation. This area of the facility is at least three times larger and far better equipped than what the former medics recalled. The group moved on to the pathology laboratories where the students study the hundred of bacteria and organisms, which cause sickness and disease in the countries they will possibly operate. A wave of astonishment overcame the visitors in this room, a room equipped with the latest microscopes, one for every student! This was like a dream to the visitors, who recall having to beg, borrow and steal to obtain such pieces of equipment. Everyone was in awe of the sophistication and even envious of the level of training the students were receiving. All of them were ready to start training again!

The most poignant and memorable moment occurred as the group left the building to walk through the inner compound area to observe the outdoor training areas. Several groups of students were practicing first aid and combat wound treatment exercises. As the visitors emerged from inside, the students stopped what they were doing—for just a split second—and gazed in wonderment at the men they had heard about. The lessons they were being taught, now stood before them. The 'old' warriors stared back—the past meeting its future. Despite this generation gap and the advancements in technology, there remains one common thread among SF medics—their ability to improvise and create a way to accomplish any task or mission.

The group was next shown some items fashioned by the students to meet the demands of the austere conditions their operating environment will require of them. Among them, leg splints created from small sections of rigid plastic, connected with combat tape to make them foldable, lightweight and small enough to fit in a rucksack. Another item, in the process of becoming patented, a suction device created by using small lengths of tubing and syringes that typically can be found in every medic's bag. The ever-resourceful medics had taken those pieces and created a device that can be used to extract fluid built up inside the chest cavity. Their resourcefulness was never ending. The tour then proceeded to the facility's library. This was another unheard of resource the visitors never had. There were computers lining two walls; each occupied by a student who had the latest medical information at his fingertips. Much like the rest of the tour, each new and improved facet witnessed, was counter balanced with a well remembered training experience. Ironically, the first thing that everyone noticed was the student sitting at a table, books open—sound asleep. He never stirred. There was laughter and joking about 'learning by osmosis' and 'meditative learning skills'; but it was a respectful, knowing laughter. He was not being laughed at—they were laughing with him, for they all knew the utterly exhausted, bone tired feeling from hours of study, attending class and, at times, as much adult beverage consumption that could be squeezed into a single day.

The tour culminated with a look through the Company D hallways. The walls are covered with the previous graduating class pictures. Hanging from the ceilings are cloth banners, made by the previous groups of students. These cleverly designed testaments from the previous classes display their remarkable achievements and the individuality of each class. Sadly, missing are many of the class pictures from the 1950's and 1960's. Indicative of the times in which Special Forces was growing, there was just never a concerted effort or standard procedure for recording the history of these men who have passed through the barracks and classrooms of Ft. Sam Houston and Ft. Bragg's medical training cycles. The veterans never really looked at their time here as a moment in history—what 21-year-old training for war does? Their accomplishments and contributions will be recorded. Their efforts were not in vain. Old photos stashed away, were promised to the Center, so they could take their rightful place among all the 'Docs'—to be forever remembered as—'Sweet M……F……!'

PART I

DAMNED GOOD MEDICS

CHAPTER 1

UNCONVENTIONAL THINKING

To appreciate the unique role of the Special Forces medic, an understanding of guerrilla, or unconventional warfare (UW) and counterinsurgency assists in gaining an insight to the overall mission of Special Forces (SF). It is only fitting that this story begins with a few quotes from the father of Special Forces Colonel Aaron Bank. Colonel Bank stated the mission and role in a personal letter "Their basic and traditional mission was to conduct all aspects of unconventional warfare deep in enemy or enemy controlled areas. Specifically, the 'A' Team's primary mission is to infiltrate deep into enemy territory…organize, train, equip, direct and when necessary, lead the indigenous guerrilla potential in its sector."[13] This was the original concept and doctrine of the Special Forces role, very reminiscent of the OSS (Office of Strategic Services) operations of World War II. This doctrine changed and evolved toward counter guerrilla and insurgency activities in Vietnam. Banks also shared his thoughts and opinion about this change. "What Special Forces did in Vietnam was to conduct a mix of conventional warfare, long range reconnaissance and a smattering of guerrilla operation and this they did damn well."[14]

Unconventional military units throughout the history of the United States have played a role in the eventual development of Special Forces. Relying on "hit and run" tactics. Superior intelligence, target surveillance, strenuous security and surprise attacks utilizing familiar terrain and the support of the local population have been the tried and true methods of many American tacticians. They were able to either defeat a much larger force or at least divert larger enemy elements to attempt countering operations to protect rear area support and communications. Thereby, reducing the enemy's ability to employ forces in offensive operations. The American Indians provide an example of the resources expended by the U.S. Army in attempting to contain small bands of Indians raiding settlements and avoiding decisive battles, forcing large numbers of U.S. troops to be deployed. Incidentally, the arrowhead on the Special Forces unit patch represents the Native American heritage in Special Forces history.

Some of the more notable unconventional warfare tacticians practicing this art form wee Major Robert Rogers during the French and Indian Wars and Lieutenant Colonel Francis Marion and his irregulars in the Carolinas, during the Revolutionary War. The Civil War exploits of Confederate John Singleton Mosby and William Quantrell may be one of the better examples of how a small group of trained soldiers can wreak havoc behind enemy lines. Raiding Union camps, destroying railway and communications lines, confiscating supplies and gathering intelligence marked their campaigns. The Union Army was forced to divert almost 50,000 men to counter these guerrilla activities. Almost 100 years later, Special Forces teams in Southeast Asia, notably the once 'Top Secret' Military Assistance Command Vietnam—Studies and Observations Group (MACV-SOG) program carried this tactic to new heights and caused the North Vietnamese Army much distress.

The U.S. Army Special Forces trace their history, not only to the warriors fighting on U.S. soil, but to those who served overseas in the OSS (Office of Strategic Services). In 1941, President Roosevelt directed William 'Wild Bill' Donovan, a tough, smart World War I Medal of Honor recipient on the Western Front, to form the Coordinator of Intelligence (COI). With operational sites in England, North Africa, India and Burma, in 1941, the agency was renamed the OSS, with Major General William Donovan in command. The OSS mission in Europe often required parachuting three (3) man 'Jedburgh Teams' into

France, Belgium and Holland, to train partisan forces and conduct guerrilla operations against German occupiers, in preparation for the D-Day invasion forces.

The OSS encountered stiff resistance from the Allied Military High Command. However, Donovan's close personal relationship with President Roosevelt enabled him to cut through military red tape and professional jealousies. The volunteers who joined the OSS had a dislike for the rigid straight-laced conventional military. These men and like minded individuals created the core group of leaders and volunteers who would later form the 10th Special Forces Group (Airborne). Much like their predecessors they later encountered the same resistance and professional jealousies in activating Special Forces.

When the Soviets broke the United States monopoly on nuclear power and blockaded Berlin, military leaders were convinced that Joseph Stalin's Soviet forces would attack in Europe by 1954. The Army again began to consider the merits of guerrilla warfare in 1951. Concealed within the Pentagon's Psychological Operations Staff Section was the new Special Warfare Division. General Robert McClure commanded this new division, consisting of a small group of men who knew the value of guerrilla warfare operations. A virtual 'Who's Who' of unconventional warfare personalities comprised the nucleus. Wendell Fertig, an American guerrilla leader on Mindanao in the Philippines. Russell Volkman, who had escaped the Bataan Death March along with Donald Blackburn and had worked with organizing that island's resistance to the Japanese. Aaron Bank, who had parachuted into occupied France and Indochina with the OSS. Joe Waters, of Merrill's Marauders and OSS fame and Robert McDowell, and OSS operative in Yugoslavia, along with other unconventional warfare volunteers, gradually defined the mission—to develop a concept and a guerrilla warfare plan for the impending World War III.

Colonel Bank formulated guidelines to train future generations of unconventional warfare warriors. During this time, based on his experiences, the Special Forces medical specialist became an important part of the unconventional warfare mission. Bank "was determined to eliminate one major flaw in the conduct of support for unconventional warfare operations. That flaw was in the area of medical aid and support."[15] This flaw could seriously impede and compromise a mission's success. Bank's also noted "that many of the guerrillas I had organized had latent fear of the consequences of getting wounded in action because of the lack of proper and immediate medical support. This in turn affected their morale."[16] That would be well illustrated in years to come. The devotion and trust that existed among Special Forces and the indigenous troops they worked with, illustrates the faith between people who knew they would be cared for if injured or in need. It was a relationship that few have experienced.

There was strong opposition to the formation of a unit specializing in this type of warfare. However, the Army Chief of Staff, General J. Lawton Collins, was receptive to the idea. With his support and General McClure's ties to the White House the Army allotted 2,500 personnel spaces for the new program in early 1952.

> "The Army Special Forces was alive. It was born out of a fear of the universally expected WW III and Soviet strength in Europe, bitter experience in Korea, inter-service rivalry, and the beliefs and determination of a handful of proponents."[17]

The 10th Special Forces Group (Airborne) was formally activated June 11, 1952 at Fort Bragg, North Carolina. It was a 'hush-hush' outfit and "an outgrowth of the military planning of the Cold War Era. In case of general or limited war, the captive nations of Eastern Europe, as well as other nations under communist dominance, presented a fertile resistance potential for military exploitation."[18]

CHAPTER 2

GROUP FORMATION

Within the ranks of the United States armed forces were future Special Forces soldiers. Many already served in the Army, Marine Corps and Air Force as medics, radio repairmen, and parachute-riggers and aircraft systems technicians. They were drawn to the new unit for the same reasons their predecessors had been drawn to the OSS. The desire to be a part of something unique, special and challenging. The men of Special Forces are triple volunteers. They volunteered to join the military, they volunteered to become airborne qualified and they volunteered for Special Forces. This brought experienced, dedicated and mature soldiers together.

An example of the high level of combat experienced men joining Special Forces was that of Sergeant Major (SGM) Julius 'Dutch' Wyngaert. 'Dutch' participated in four combat jumps with 82nd Airborne during World War; the invasion of Sicily, Italy, Normandy and Holland. He was among the first to join the new unit in 1952 as a demolition's specialist, then changed in 1956 to become a medical specialist. 'Dutch' received medical training while stationed in Wurzburg, Germany with the 10th Group. This was during the development of the initial medical training program for the Special Forces medic. The course, coupled with On the Job Training (OJT) at a hospital in Nuremburg, lasted approximately three months. Once the training was completed he was not officially awarded the MOS (Military Occupational Skill), but acted in the dual capacity of medic/demolition's. When he returned to Ft. Bragg, North Carolina in the late 1950's, he was sent to Ft. Sam Houston Texas for further medical schooling. He then returned to Ft. Bragg for more OJT at Womack Army Hospital.

There were no rigid standards for completion of training for medics. Wyngaert was pulled out of Womack on three separate occasions for field training exercises, before completing the full ten weeks of OJT. The fourth time he was removed from the middle of training at Womack was for deployment to Laos with the first SF teams for Operation 'HOTFOOT'. This type of experience was repeated over and over with many of the initial medics.[19]

Colonel Bank, the 10th Group's first commander, designated an E-7, Sergeant First Class (SFC), and position for an enlisted medic[20] in each Special Forces operational detachment. There were no "particular requirements for the single enlisted medic."[21] Bank was adamant on one point—each team was to contain "damned good medics!"[22] This requirement was essential based on "…the absence of any organic medical capability, often resulted in needless death and suffering among OSS operatives."[23] He further defined the operational role of the enlisted medic in an UW situation.

> "His assignment was to carry out the normal aidman functions, develop an indigenous medical network in the team's sector, plan and supervise their training and physical setup. Establish clandestine methods of transporting casualties, setting up safe houses, storage and distribution of supplies."[24]

Colonel Bank's statements convey the enormous amount of responsibility that would be required of the enlisted Special Forces medic. Bank also emphasized the importance of training and why the medic would need above average skills and knowledge.

> "Admittedly, in under developed countries indigenous medical personnel would usually not be available and the aidman would be more or less on his own, but in Europe they would be, always remembering that the anticipated area of operations for Special Forces would be behind the Iron Curtain…even in these areas it might be difficult to develop a medical net. The

requirement arose that the Special Forces aidman be as professionally competent as possible."[25]

Later, men such as Alan Maggio, Coy Melton, Edward Montgomery, Manfred Baier, Carey Drumheller, Paul Campbell, Earle Peckham and Ned Miller would help make Colonel Banks' vision a reality. They and many others were the first stepping stones for future generations of medics to follow. Many contributed more than just their medical skills. For example, Coy Melton served in every capacity on Special Forces teams, Paul Campbell became an operations and intelligence NCO. Some, such as Al Maggio and Larry Dickinson spent almost their entire career in Special Forces as a medic.

CHAPTER 3
UNCONVENTIONAL TRAINING

The men who gathered on Smoke Bomb Hill in Ft. Bragg were, unbeknownst to them, beginning a long and proud tradition. They would take part in events that shaped the history of Special Forces and of our Nation. Their experiences led to changes in training and vindicated the requirement that Special Forces soldiers must be comprised of men possessing the highest levels of intelligence, training and dedication to meet the demands of an ever-evolving mission. Al Maggio recalled having to "sign a statement that they had volunteered for Special Forces Training, volunteered for Basic Airborne Training, if they were not already qualified, and volunteered to go behind enemy lines if necessary. Further processing included obtaining background checks to clear them for eligibility to handle and receive classified information and training."[26]

The desirability to have the highest caliber persons available created a need for selection criteria to predict probable performance in an operational setting. Once a team has been deployed on a mission, it was too late to find out that an individual could place the mission and the rest of his team members in jeopardy. In 1990 Major Louis Dorogi described this requirement:

> "Exhaustive studies combined standard psychological measurement techniques with the 'effectiveness' criteria generated by Special Forces. The findings highlighted a need for older, mature personnel possessing the necessary physical stamina

> and showing a preference for non-routine, outdoor work, as well as specific rejection of detailed busy work. Other indices developed by the studies showed that there was a higher probability of effectiveness among those with a past willingness to assume family and community responsibility and among those who didn't ascribe any particular glamour of excitement to their occupation."[27]

Elite status always seemed to create jealousy and resentment among traditional military officials. Thus, began the long internal struggles for Special Forces to establish, expand and maintain this vital role. Paul Campbell, on of the earlier SF medics, remembers the struggle during Special Forces infancy; "The high ranking officers of the U.S. Army couldn't buy into the SF type of operations. They felt we were mavericks with no military bearing and our tactics would not work in actual operations."[28] This prevailing attitude toward Special Forces posed a bevy of problems for the medics. Campbell recalled that, "Most conventional unit commanders didn't want anything to do with SF and the medical facilities, at that time, they were not prepared for the utilization of the services of an enlisted PA (Physician Assistant) type. Back in those days most of us got in-house training by each other and a lot of us got a chance to work on OJT (On the Job Training) at Womack Army Medical Center at Bragg and the regular training [combat medic] at Fort Sam Houston."[29]

Maggio reflected further on those early experiences.

> "The beginnings of the finest medic the Army could produce were trying for the Army's Medical Department to accept, the Airborne Medical Doctors and Medical Service Corps Officers who would spend countless hours devising the concepts and doctrine for how these medics who were to be trained and implemented into the newly formed unit."[30]

To offset the lack of a structured higher command element for the medics, a medical detachment was included within the Group

Headquarters. Its Surgeon acted in the same capacity as that of a Regimental Surgeon.

> "But slanted to the guerrilla and clandestine field requirements of Special Forces...The Group Surgeon would be the medical support for the operating teams. He would supervise the medical training and employment of the Group's medical personnel at the Group base locations, but their Special Forces operation training would be handled by their team commanders, since all team members were cross trained."[31]

Colonel Bank realized the task was enormous for developing a training system. It would require specialized training, exceeding that of the typical aidman. Current training was not going to suffice to meet the special needs of unconventional warfare. Requirements were developed "giving only minimum consideration to the limitations imposed by the lack of formal medical education of the unit's aidman."[32]

The first Army Medical Department (AMEDD) officer to be assigned to Special Forces, First Lieutenant Robert E. Elliott, MSC (Medical Service Corps) arrived at Ft. Bragg, July 18, 1952. He became the first to have a tremendous impact on the development of medical training. Elliott worked with Colonel Bank and his staff to develop the training program for the needs of the Special Forces medic. The result was the Medical Aidman's Course. Once the medical training had been formulated, they were submitted to the Pentagon. Bank detailed the next steps for creation of the new training. "They [higher command elements] contacted the medical center at Ft. Sam Houston and arrangements were made to afford a broader and more professional medical course for our aidman...since late 1952 all initial medical training for Special Forces was conducted here."[33] In future years, the Chief Medical Aidman's Course, eventually became the mid-level course (F-300) conducted at Ft. Sam Houston for SF medics. The academic challenge the course presented was by far, the toughest and most intense instruction ever received by attendees. Even forty to fifty years later, the medics who attended the course credit its rigorous demands for enabling them to achieve their aspirations for further education and success in everything.

No time was wasted getting the program underway. A weekly Activities Report, dated October 11, 1952, issued from the Psychological Warfare Center, just four months after the formation of the 10th Group, outlines the first recorded training for medics. Beginning October 13, 1952, an advanced cadre-training course with emphasis placed on communications and medical instruction was begun. Less than a month later, another Weekly Activities Report dated November 8, 1952, stated that preparations will be made to send 28 enlisted men to attend the Chief Medical Aidman Course at Ft. Sam Houston, Texas. Two weeks later, another report documented that the official beginning for medical training commenced on or around November 22, 1952 when twenty-eight (28) enlisted men departed for Ft. Sam Houston, Texas.

The development of the standardization for medical training did not necessarily dictate the sequence of training. Since many of the initial members of 10th Group had considerable combat medical experience, unconventional warfare training often took precedence. This is evident from an aged, yellowing piece of paper. Special Order 127, dated November 6, 1952, Headquarters, Psychological Warfare Center placed men on TDY (Temporary Duty) to attend Special Forces training for eight weeks, effective November 10, 1952. Among them were medics Edward L. Montgomery, Lindsay F. Fant, William K Cole, Meeland F. Francis, Paul Vucovich and Johnny W. Jones. The names, compliments of Sergeant Major Edward L. Montgomery, represent just some of the medics who were a part of the 10th Special Forces Group.

These men had participated in WW II as combat medics and were deemed trained medics, for the time being, even though the official first class of other medics were assigned to Ft. Sam medical training. Montgomery recalled, "The majority of us were well trained in our MOS at the time. The criteria that we had for the medics to be assigned was that they had to have the medical badge or combat experience, preferably they wanted them from the infantry field with combat parachute jumps."[34] 'Monty' had acquired the prerequisites during both World War II and Korea.

As training commenced at Ft. Sam Houston, there was a resistance to the 'unconventional' medical training for Special Forces medics. A preponderance of the physicians assigned to train SF medics were reluctant to teach advanced surgical procedures to enlisted personnel. Some of this was overcome by First Lieutenant Elliot's efforts to familiarize the physicians with the Special Forces operational concept. Colonel Bank remembered that the nature of guerrilla warfare precluded the restrictions of stateside medicine. "The prevailing philosophy was that the enlisted personnel were, in essence, physician substitutes in a general warfare situation. Operational necessity dictated that these levels of training, that of which only medical students received, were limited, but the focus for such sophisticated training for enlisted personnel was justified."[35] The lives of the team members depended on the team medic because evacuation of wounded team members from behind enemy lines would likely not be an option. For example, procedures such as emergency appendectomies were exhaustively explained and emphasized to provide the medic with the knowledge to identify the problem and take necessary measures in the event circumstances dictated a need to operate on a team member or a guerrilla fighter. Paul Campbell recalls the resistance to train NCO's in such techniques.

> "I remember the training tried to keep us restricted to typical ward medic, bed pans, etc. But we needed more and seeked out more instructions in emergency room procedures, etc. We wanted to get hands on delivery training, but were limited to training films. I also remember trying to get doctors to let us do more in emergency room treatments and some gave us additional duties but in most cases if that doctor was not on duty the head nurse on duty or another doctor would restrict our duties to 'medic'. There was a time that we couldn't even be present in a delivery room or examine an American female patient or for that matter, a full examination of a male patient."[36]

After training was completed at Ft. Sam Houston, the medics returned to Ft. Bragg and assigned to duties at Womack Army Hospital. This procedure was a forerunner to OJT (On the Job Training). Under supervision of a physician, the medics screened patients, for their symptoms, took their temperature and blood pressure. The doctor then saw patients, and in most cases, the medic was initially not allowed to be present during full examination. In the emergency room, they received a little more hands-on experience, but were still limited in what they could do to a patient. Campbell explained the medics' developing relationships with the medical professionals.

> "As some of the doctors got to know us and our SF mission, they worked closer with us in our hands on training needs. The nurses at the time were very restrictive because they were accountable for our ward duties when on their shift, and we surely couldn't do anything they themselves were not allowed to do."[37]

The professional jealousies and the lack of medical staff's understanding of unconventional warfare operations contributed to some difficulties between the medics and their trainers. Al Maggio attended the courses with the second group of medics sent to Ft. Sam Houston. He recalled:

> "Upon arrival at Ft. Sam Houston, we found that during class and hospital phases there was a problem of communicating our position in the field behind enemy lines, without support of Med-Evac and the other niceties of war, such as a Battalion Aid Station, Ambulances, MASH and Field Hospitals, not to mention the US Navy Hospital ships offshore, that a stable command structure requires for the support of line troops. The instructor staff was not ready for the questions we presented in reference to utilization of equipment available and techniques of instruction. [What] they thought was all we need to know. It was unheard of to think [that] a NCO Medical Aidman would perform many medical and surgical techniques in the field,

without the Medical Department's support, after initial injuries and wounds were treated at the front lines. It was very frustrating, to say the least, for us to plead and bargain for a better course during those early phases at Ft. Sam."[38]

The exhaustive academic workload encountered at Ft. Sam Houston was compacted into a very short time period. E. Grant Madison, the second Non-Commissioned Officer In Charge (NCOIC) at the Surgical Research Lab, had this to say about the course, "It was a fast course and they put it out fast and you had to get it and burn a lot of midnight oil."[39] The skills and procedures being taught to enlisted medics were generally reserved for medical students. The intensity level of these courses, mainly human physiology, required hard work and many hours of study. Carey Drumheller remembered:

> "Ft. Sam was primarily all classroom. We used the Merck Manual, Gray's Anatomy and Surgery of the Ambulatory Patient as our principal books and study guides. If you were failing, you were history. The word was that if you failed, you would lose a stripe when you got back to the unit…If I remember correctly, it was eight weeks, five days a week, eight hours a day of the most intensive training I had ever had, college or otherwise. Professional Army doctors and nurses staffed the school and they did not cut you any slack. You were treated like a third year medical student at college, but boy did you learn a lot."[40]

Ft. Sam Houston academics were brutal for good reason. Not only were these men being trained in advanced medical procedures typically reserved for medical professionals, they would also need to maintain a calm composure to perform them under extremely stressful conditions. The academics provided an important test not only of this knowledge but also their maturity. The program tested their ability and reliability. Once a medic was deployed with a team was not the time to find out whether he would be able to put the training to use. Dr. Roger A. Juel, MC, a surgeon involved with SF medics during the early years, stated that "You can be an academic genius and it will not let you out of this course. And when you are going to trust a man with the information that physician with years of training has, if we trust him with that information, if he is not reliable, he is not getting out of here. Failure is not academic by any means."[41] Reliability is based on performance. The medic must have the ability to recognize his own limitations, the ability to work with those limitations and seek assistance when he doesn't know how to handle something. In an actual operational setting that is not always possible.

For medics, the intense pressure from studying and training created a unique environment from the very beginning. Being individuals who took immense pride in their abilities, they developed a mythical and legendary reputation. These unconventional mavericks created and perpetuated an aura of mystery. The difficult classroom instruction coupled with long hours of study and being away from the restricted confines of military life at Ft. Bragg was a breeding ground for their sometimes-unorthodox behavior. In fact, their unconventional specialization demanded nothing short of original thought provoking consternation. Activities and 'oddities' included, but were not limited to, an airborne qualified pet rat, 'raids' at the Women's Army Corps barracks, also known as the WAC Shack and singing 'hymnals' for officers, kidnapping alligators and never ending contests to outwit the Military Police (MP's). An endless list of 'illicit' activities proved to be a 'thorn' for command and security elements at every turn. It is important to understand they weren't hellions bent on destruction. It was simply a release valve for the intense pressure placed on these men. These activities were also a way to communicate that they were different and unique. This particular phenomenon was part of being a Special Forces soldier.

There were several factors that contributed to this unique environment. First, at times, military staff members stationed at Ft. Sam Houston was not very supportive of such sophisticated training for non-commissioned officers. This led to 'acting out' by the medics in order to release tension, frustration and convey their displeasure with not being trained in the manner they felt appropriate. It is important to remember that it was in the very nature of the Special Forces soldier's character to have a less than favorable outlook about the Regular Army's strict spit and polish practices. The early medics did not have the same propensity for the unorthodox behavior at least during training. Perhaps they were just older and wiser. However, the need to be different did reach back into the formative years. Two medics were involved in the following news clipping from an undated Army Times article and provided a glimpse into the long history of this time honored tradition.

> "We're willing to go on record that Flint Caserne in Bad Tölz has a fine collection of characters as can be found anywhere. One feller' we saw in the snack bar the other day had his blonde hair parted on both sides with the middle section combed fetchingly over his forehead in a spit curl. Then there's the guy who wears a pink sweater, pink socks and pale green slacks. But the best of all is the guy who frightens the German librarian at 9 p.m. every night by leering at her from down the hall dressed in his—you guessed—birthday suit."[42]

CHAPTER 4

EVOLUTION BEGINS

After several years of struggling to survive and become a cohesive unit, Special Forces' innate ability to adapt to change, learn from mistakes and seek a better method resulted in a command structure that demanded specialized training for its members. Until the mid 1950's, medical training was a continuous process to upgrade their medical proficiency between tactical training missions intermingled with regular garrison duties when time permitted. The duration of the Medical Aidman course varied and were primarily targeted toward getting the student acclimated to the medical environment. The earliest documentation available indicates an official start for specific training designed for Special Forces medic's dates back to 1954. At this time, there was no course for the different requirements for Special Forces medics. An MSC (Medical Service Corps) officer, Vern Newgaard, asked the school at Ft. Sam Houston to develop a course specifically for Special Forces medics, who would have to operate independently behind enemy lines. Colonel Richard L. Coppedge (MC), was the coordinator of enlisted training at the Medical Field Service School (MFSS). Coppedge first recommended a twenty-week curriculum, which was not accepted. Eventually, an eight-week didactic course was accepted, with four additional weeks in the hospital, working in "outpatient wards, emergency room and surgical observation, if not participation."[43] The training was specifically designed for Special Forces in addition to the initial eight weeks of standard medical training previously approved. The classes were small, ten to fifteen men at most. The first class was approximately ten medics. From the start, officials from the MFSS created difficulties in approving the course material. Coppedge recalls the tremendous support received from Colonel 'Henry' [all Coppedge can recall ever calling him] from the Department of Medicine and Surgery. He helped clear the hurdles. He approved the course content "trying to get a guy like the Special Forces medic off the ground."[44] Even though Dr. 'Henry' was also not a member of Special Forces, his colorful background[45], as recalled by Coppedge, and his non-Regular Army officer demeanor most likely contributed to his support of the unorthodox Special Forces.

The biggest concern/question about the high level of the training to be given the Special Forces enlisted medic was the subject of surgery. Coppedge personally instructed the medics, upwards of 17 hours per week. In an interview with Major Dorogi, he stressed, as did Colonel Juel, that intelligence was only a requirement to become a medic.

> "It was obvious from the beginning that the problem in the training was not technique, but judgment. Here is a question of maturity and balance, keeping a cool head, knowing what to do, knowing what you could do safely. It's also a question of teaching the medic what to do in every situation, so that there was something that he could do."[46]

Paul Campbell, who joined the 77th Special Forces Group after completion of airborne training school in 1953, recalled that "in the early days, the training [medical] was hit or miss."[47] After receiving approximately eight (8) to ten (10) weeks of didactic training covering topics such as; the identification and treatment of diseases, sanitation practices, musco-skeletal anatomy, pharmaceutical and multiple types of injury treatment, the medics returned to Ft. Bragg and worked in Womack Army Hospital. Here, the medics rotated through the Emergency Room, OBGYN, Pediatric, Surgery and Post-Operative wards. Additionally, they also received training with the Group Dentist, learning how to perform fillings, extractions and the clinical specifics of gum diseases. Campbell recalled working on ward duty,

> "We rotated throughout the hospital and cared for all types of patients, but this was more as 'orderly' type work. In most cases we were under the supervision of a nurse, so you can see from this that we were at low level. Back in those days even nurses couldn't do a lot of things they do now, without a doctor's orders. This is one of the reasons I'm sure SF had to set up its own level of training in the SF lab. On sick call, the patient would be screened in by the medic, sent to the doctor, prescribed medication and/or treatment. We may get some hand on practice in giving injections and if a good doctor [was on duty] they would let us suture under their supervision."[48]

Though some advances and standardization had occurred with OJT at Womack Army Hospital it is important to remember that, at this time, once medics returned to Ft. Bragg from the didactic medical training at Ft. Sam—operational training took precedence. OJT was not yet a formalized phase of the medical training program. The ward duties were fit into the busy schedule of operational exercises. Weapons, demolitions and language training were continuous to achieve specialty cross training of all team members. Field exercises were conducted in many different climates and terrain. Campbell recalls, "the medic trained in the tactical settings such as, raids, ambushes, sabotage missions, blowing bridges, railroads, electrical systems, setting up escape and evasion (E and E) systems. Our training was along the lines of the old OSS training. Training that would prepare us to work behind enemy lines and to carry missions behind enemy lines. We were also expected to train others to perform these duties."[49]

Other medics, such as Alan B. Maggio brought valuable experience to Smoke Bomb Hill in June 1952. 'Big Al', had served during the Korean War with the 24th Recon Company as a medic. He then spent an additional 10 months on Kojedo Island off Korea, treating prisoners of war (POW's). When he joined Special Forces, he was 24 years old. He initially joined the Army in his hometown of Jamaica, New York at the age of 18. His previous medical experience made a perfect fit in his new unit. As a member of the second class to attend the Chief Medical Aidman's School at Ft. Sam, he recalls the course lasted 8 weeks. After completion, medics were sent back to Ft. Bragg for the first Medical Aidman's Course. The month long course covered amputations and diagnosis and treatments for multiple types of wounds and illnesses.

With each new class of medics, the medical training and course material changed at a rapid pace. Each successive class provided valuable feedback about course content. Without their foresight and the realization that any shortcomings in the training must be corrected, future SF medics would have been woefully unprepared to accomplish their mission. Al Maggio described the intensity of the training necessary to provide the medic with the skills to operate in an unconventional warfare setting.

> "More training was required to develop guidelines and certain ethics to utilize in future missions. This included prenatal, childbirth and postnatal care for guerrilla families. We also had to be able to instruct these methods of first aid to others through an interpreter. We received a short course of diagnosis and treatment procedures from Captain Freeland. He conducted small classes on amputation procedures being used in Korea. In small groups we processed through this phase then into the main post (old) hospital for days OJT in all the wards, *such as the OR [operating room] and ER [emergency room].* This also included childbirth observation and postnatal care at the ward level. The men finally got 'hands on' experience compared with Brooke Army Medical Hospital, where professional jealousy *among some of the nurses over requirements for such involved training created an environment that found us serving as* 'bed pan commandos'. The word got around the Army medical circles that our medics at Fort Sam Houston and Fort Bragg [Womack] Hospital were putting out honor graduates and did their share on each shift, even volunteering for extra shifts at all levels to get the experiences and the knowl-

> edge they needed before returning to an A Detachment. As the months went by, coordination between Ft. Bragg and Ft. Sam Houston's training staffs brought about a more basic understanding of the SF medical mission. Through good diplomacy and support, things smoothly fell into step."[50]

As time progressed and fewer combat experienced men entered the ranks of Special Forces medics, men like Carey Drumheller benefited greatly from the foresight of previous medics and the resulting changes made to the training. Drumheller, a medic with the newly formed 10th Special Forces Group, enlisted in the Army with an airborne commitment on September 3, 1952. During Basic Training at Ft. Riley, Kansas, as part of a group of five or six men whose records had apparently been screened for physical condition and test scores from the induction test, Drumheller remembers being asked, "to volunteer for this new unit. We were told that we would receive UDT (Underwater Demolitions Training), parachute and Ranger type training, and all that 'stuff' sounded like fun."[51] After completing jump school at Ft. Benning, Georgia in February 1953, they boarded a bus and ended up on Smoke Bomb Hill at Ft. Bragg. Later, they found out they had been put on orders for Special Forces in November 1952. Drumheller was astonished;

> "I had volunteered for SF…I had no idea what I was getting into…the training was immediate and intense. Military Mountaineering at Camp Carson Colorado, Marine Raider School at the Naval Amphibious Landing School in Little Creek Virginia, psychological warfare, weapons and anything else they could think of."[52]

This example reflects that during the formative years of Special Forces, the selection and training process was somewhat random. In the not so distant future the selection process became based primarily on test scores and/or previous college education. This was especially true for the Special Forces medic. As the pool of men possessing prior training and service as combat medics during World War II and Korea became reduced, it became imperative that a uniform training process be developed. Some of the medics simply chose their specialty, recalls Drumheller, when asked by the personnel office, as to "what I wanted to be when I grew up."[53] Drumheller had a choice and chose to be a medic, thinking that it would benefit him throughout life. "I was correct, I raised four boys and a girl and practiced medicine on all of them at one time or another, while they were growing up."[54]

The uniformity of training courses provided a common means to successfully complete the same training before being awarded the MOS identifier for a Special Forces medic. During the Clinical Aidman's Course taught at Ft. Bragg, the medics learned bandaging techniques, splinting procedures and sterile procedures, the names of surgical instruments and supplies for use in specific instances, all under the supervision of the Group Surgeon. They also worked on various wards at the hospital.

Through Drumheller's experiences the evolution of the level of training can be seen. It was slow to change and demanded better training and exposure to real situations. Drumheller's recollection of garrison duty and OJT at Ft. Bragg describes the environment in which medics gained valuable medical experience. "Payday weekends provided a lot of trauma experience with car wrecks and bar fights providing the patients."[55] Inventiveness was pervasive among the medics. Drumheller recalled the finer uses for medical equipment, demonstrating that Special Forces had the ability to use items on hand to quickly resolve an issue. Duties at Womack included sterilization and packaging of surgical instruments using the autoclave. Additionally, but equally important, was learning "how to cook midnight snacks in the autoclave when you had overnight duty."[56] Drumheller also provided an example of how far medicine has come since his time in Special Forces. As a student, one of their duties was to "sharpen needles by dragging the needle across an oil stone and then check it for burrs by pulling it through cotton."[57]

Some of the ward duties presented the new medic with situations, which really tested them to see if they possessed the 'right stuff'. Drumheller remembers working on the Dermatology Ward where the unpleasant and persistent odor of burn patients permeated everything. The duty helped to determine if an individual was prepared to deal with the serious injuries and illnesses they could expect to encounter. The medics also assisted doctors in surgery, such as the removal of a femur nail. A femur nail, which is literally a big nail, is placed inside of the femur when it is completely broken. Once healed, the nail is removed. This was done using an instrument that looks like a cross between a dent puller for an automobile and a claw hammer. The claws are hooked over the head of the nail. A weight is slid up the handle against the stop, to pull the nail out. Drumheller recalls his experience.

> "I had to get at the foot end of the operating table, get the patient by the foot and pull and twist at the direction of the two doctors who were having a difficult time removing the nail. They were sweating and their masks kept falling down. The nurses were about to have kittens trying to preserve a sterile field and I was marveling at the Anglo Saxon language the doctors were capable of."[58]

As a young medic in training, Drumheller faced many tests to his resolve to complete the training. For instance, the possibility of a medic having to assist or perform the duties of delivering a baby was very real in an operational area. To prepare for this, the medics received familiarization training with the birth process. They worked in the Obstetrics ward (OB) observing and sometimes, depending on the doctor, helping to deliver babies, Drumheller remembered that, "it was at this point I could have become a monk, because I swore off sex forever…almost!"[59]

From its humble beginnings and an 'ad hoc' approach, born of necessity and driven by dedication, the medical training of Special Forces had created a unique breed of men, trained in unprecedented manner to meet the challenges of a changing world. The lessons learned had immeasurable impact on those that were there in the beginning and on countless others who followed in their footsteps.

CHAPTER 5
GROUP EXPANSION

The unorthodox and challenging training procedures were slowly developing for medics as Special Forces was expanding. In September of 1953, the 77th Special Forces Group was formed at Ft. Bragg from core members of the 10th Group, before the 10th Group shipped out for their new home in Bad Tölz Germany. Just prior to the 10th Group's deployment to Bad Tölz, First Lieutenant William Freeland, MC was assigned as the new Group Surgeon. The medics in Germany soon benefited from realistic and practical training due to two significant factors. First, Lieutenant Freeland was thoroughly dedicated to ensuring the medical preparedness of Special Forces. Second, stateside medical restrictions were not a factor in the military hospitals and dispensaries in Germany. Lt. Freeland contributed significantly to the development of the medics training. 'Doc' Freeland worked to create an OJT program, that established and maintained medical proficiency at selected hospitals in Munich, Ansbach, Hohenfels and Grafenwohr. The medics also received, at these locations, about two months of sophisticated training in surgical procedures. The effort and dedication from Doc Freeland, in conjunction with the participating medical facilities, provided the hands on training needed to complement the didactic training received in the United States.

Carey Drumheller was among those who went to Bad Tölz. 'Drum' recalls Doc Freeland with fondness and admiration, "I think Doc had been in civilian practice in a small town somewhere in the hill country of an eastern state. He was an outstanding instructor, not just treatment, but in patient relationships. He once told the story of an old Grandma bringing her teenage granddaughter to him for treatment of a carbuncle[60] under the girl's arm."[61] Drumheller noted Doc Freeland's patient interaction philosophy and its relation to Special Forces medical mission.

> "Doc had been making attempts to entice the 'hill' people to come to him for medical needs, but these folks relied principally on 'home remedies' supplied by the matriarch of the family. Grandma had been treating the carbuncle with a fresh cow patty poultice. No kidding. Doc said that after the girl was cleaned up he lanced the carbuncle, shot the girl full of antibiotics, and a tetanus shot. He then told Grandma that she had done a great job and if she would give the girl these pills for a week and bring her back they would see how '*their*' [he and Grandma's] treatment had worked. A valuable lesson for later SF medics. Never insult an attempt to do good within a certain culture or population regardless of how primitive. Be their friend first and then their doctor. Doc said that after that he started getting more of the hill folks as patients. His classes were something you actually looked forward to. Question: Doc, I have a man who is shot through the stomach, internal bleeding, peritonitis, low blood pressure and going into shock. We are 200 miles from the nearest doctor or hospital, and in enemy territory. He is going to die, what am I going to do—operate or let him die? Doc's typical reply, Operate and do your best, he will at least have a chance. If he dies, just remember that you did not kill him, the bullet did."[62]

Drumheller recalled another occasion for a typical Doc Freeland response during obstetrics' class, one of the men remarked that he had no intention of delivering babies. Doc's reply was classic, 'son, if you are there when she is ready, you *will* deliver the baby, want to or not."[63] Edward Montgomery also recalled Doc Freeland as, "A fine individual, understood our problems, went out of his way to aid us in every way he could."[64]

Another surgeon who was very helpful to Special Forces was Dr. Baker, an Orthopedic Surgeon. Unfortunately, Montgomery doesn't recall his first name, but remembers well the support in allowing the medic to sit with him during an initial examination of a patient. Afterwards, he would describe and explain the specific procedures he was going to use during the operation. Along with the doctor, the medics scrubbed as operating room assistants and "a lot of the cavities he would let us close, especially the *synovial* cavities. Very, very interesting—I think we gained quite a bit from it all."[65]

Drumheller felt that the resistance to providing advanced medical training for enlisted men was due to the hospital staff "not knowing the whole story *behind the reason and mission Special Forces medics would be expected to perform such advanced medical procedures.* There was conflict between us and some of the younger nurses. We would hold retractors, clip bleeders, tie off, cut-off viscera and suture. We did as the doctors directed and some, but not all, of the younger nurses resented a corporal or a staff sergeant working on a patient when they couldn't but they still had to hand us the instruments we wanted. I don't mean to imply that everyone was like that, but there were a few."[66]

The training objectives at the 2nd Field Hospital, located in Munich Germany, were primarily geared toward 'hands on' surgical training. "On hernia operations I often got to sew up the last couple of layers of skin. We did reductions, which is a fracture with the bone sticking through the skin…I often got to help on these."[67] Drumheller provides a unique insight about the subsequent additional training in Germany with fewer restrictions placed on medical training.

> "We were broken down into provisional companies of FA teams. I was in FA 15, 3rd Provisional Company. I did my surgical training at the 2nd Field Hospital in Munich Germany. At the time, Colonel Shrum was Chief of Surgery and Major Gilpatrick, Assistant Chief of Surgery. Both were career Army Doctors, neither was Special Forces. Two medics would be assigned to them for surgical OJT. We did everything with

> the doctors except operations on dependents and most serious cases."[68]

Another medic, Manfred Baier, arrived in Bad Tölz, back to his homeland of Germany, in January 1955 and had almost identical experiences:

> "The training I received was especially great during my assignment with the 10th SFGA [Special Forces Group (Airborne)] in Germany. During my time there, in addition to the various cross specialty training I received, I attended many hours of classroom work within the unit it detailed anatomy and physiology of the human body, pharmacology, emergency medical procedures etc. While at OJT for eight weeks with 2nd Field Hospital, Munich, the Chief of Surgery that we, the SF medics especially, worked as scrub nurses and assistant surgeons during general surgical procedures in actual surgery cases. I also had the opportunity to work with the orthopedic surgeon...Broken bones and other injuries were common in airborne units."[69]

Although the new surroundings, with fewer restrictions on medical training procedures, they were still plagued, but not hindered or deterred, by the usual resistance that seemed to follow Special Forces. Drumheller recalled one occasion of being confronted by a Regular Army Officer concerning the 'not yet official' beret on his head. After attending a Board of Review for Helicopter School, he and two other fellow SF'ers had left the Headquarters building wearing their Class A uniforms complete with their berets. He described the events that followed.

> "As I was leaving the HQ building, I put on my headgear [beret]. I met a Captain along the way and saluted him. He stopped me, and as I turned around, he stood me at attention and proceeded to chew me out for wearing an unauthorized [piece of] headgear and made me remove it [the beret] from

> my head. The Captain had his back to the entrance of the HQ building. Over his shoulder, I saw our Group Adjutant, Lt. Colonel Corl, come out the HQ door and walk toward us. He had his Beret on! I knew I had been saved! Colonel Corl walked up and asked the Captain if there was a problem. I thought the Captain would faint when he saw the Colonel with a Beret on! I was dismissed and as the three of us drove off, the Colonel was having a 'chat' with the Captain."[70]

During the early part of 1954, the need for medical instruction overseas heralded a Clinical Aidman's Class that was developed by the 10th Special Forces Group and taught in Flint Kaserne, Germany. The students in Germany like the medics attending training at Ft. Sam Houston also used the *Merck Manual* and *Ferguson's Surgery of the Ambulatory Patient.* Edward Montgomery finished the Clinical Aidman and OJT portion of training on February 11, 1954. He recalls a few of the enlisted medical instructors he received training from; Jerry Richardson, 'Fish' Restall, Pope, Moore, Cullford, Murray, Licon, Cole, Knox and Worthington. The sequence which Montgomery received official training is interesting, in that he was an original medic who joined Special Forces on the very first day of it's existence and here he was, two years later, still attending qualification courses. This was not an unusual practice. It is indicative of the level of training that all medics received. Even though they were technically qualified, because most were combat experienced medics, they were always searching for ways to increase their knowledge and skills.

The newly arrived 10th Group members also continued tactical training for the anticipated invasion of Europe by Soviet forces. Training never ceased and the medics were a part of the overall team. They had a vital dual role as healer and combatant. Robert J. Leonpacher, a classmate of Drumheller's joined Special Forces in April 1953. In a letter, he discussed the aspects of the military training and skills that were required of the medics. His ability to speak fluent German (his father was a German cavalryman before coming to the United States) often placed him in the position of conducting plain-clothes reconnaissance during field exercises in Germany. Leonpacher depicts the responsibilities of the medic as a soldier, and how Special Forces was to blend into their surroundings and operate behind enemy lines by enlisting the help of the local people.

> "One of our ski exercises on the mountain just southwest of Bad Tölz, Benedictenbaum. I was transported with a horse drawn sled with cases of C-rations to this little alpine resort. There were three or four of us, don't remember who the other guys were. We had to guard the rations till the troops came by and then continue on with them. We slept in our down-lined sleeping bags upstairs on what was really just a wide shelf. We paid fifty cents a night so we didn't have to sleep outside. We bought our meals and beer from the people probably for only two or three marks…After three days we handed out the rations and joined our team and continued the next day and a half on the exercise."[71]

Leonpacher also offered some insight into the inherent dangers and medical emergencies that were encountered while training in adverse and rugged terrain.

> "When we made a three day ski trek there were a lot of ankle and leg injuries. Everyone was taken out using skis lashed together. There were no helicopters available, and the Weasels [tracked snow vehicle] could not get up to where we were. We probably had twenty-five percent of the guys not finish the three days."[72]

CHAPTER 6
TEAM MEMBER

The dual role of warrior and healer is perhaps what makes the Special Forces medic the most unique member of the Special Forces team. He is responsible for the team's health and welfare and is also capable of participating in small unit military operations. This combination means he will be treated as a combatant, not a medic, by enemy forces and not accorded the protections applied to medical personnel in accordance with the agreements in the Geneva Convention. Drumheller aptly defines what was expected. "Just because you were a medic didn't mean that you would never have to climb a mountain, row a rubber raft, blow up a bridge or organize an ambush."[73] This philosophy of cross training all team members created a backup if for any reason the designated combat specialist was unable to perform. Drumheller adds, "I could set up and ANGR [pronounced 'anger', also referred too as 'angry'] 9 radio and communicate with whomever. But, I could not send and receive Morse code [referred to as 'dit-dot-dit'] as good as our radio operator. On the other hand he could not perform surgical techniques as good as I could, but he could probably stop the bleeding and save your life."[74]

The overall team mission was never secondary. The medic is a part of the team, requiring him to be prepared to conduct combat operations in addition to his medical responsibilities. Al Maggio describes the emphasis on tactical training.

> "Upon return to Ft. Bragg, we were assigned to an A Detachment to begin our Special Forces Basic Training Course. Here, we learned how we would be employed in the field supporting a

Unconventional Warfare Unit at Company and Battalion level. Tactics utilizing raid and ambush techniques that had been successfully carried out in previous wars. We studied historical events that had used partisans and watched films in classrooms with security doubled on the street and guards at the doors. We were also taught how to operate US and Russian weapons. After demolition indoctrination and training in the use of various types of demolition's and devices we learned how to implement them in the field by actually detonating several types of different explosives. Field radio use was not taught to us at this time, but team integrity and employment was used on two or three field problems before the 10th Group deployed to Germany."[75]

The full range of training that all medics underwent in their medical specialty and also as a combat soldier is further underscored by the experiences of Manfred Baier, nicknamed 'Yogi' and sometimes 'Kraut', because of his German heritage. Baier came to the United States as a quota immigrant, when his uncle in California agreed to be his sponsor. He left his homeland, because he felt Germany held no promise for his future. His sense of adventure carried him to the new land. He worked on some family farms before being drafted into the Army on February 15, 1953 exactly eight months to the day after his arrival in the United States. At the age of 23 he joined the 77th Special Forces Group and attended the medical and tactical training cycles, as well as getting airborne qualified. The intense amount of training consolidated into such short periods of time is impressive. During his service with the 10th Group from 1955 to 1959 he traveled to Oberammergau Germany for Radio Operator Intelligence Specialist [Hungarian language] training. He attended the 7th US Army Non-Commissioned Officers School. After returning from Germany he was assigned first to the 77th, then the 7th and finally the 5th Special Forces Groups. From 1959 to 1961 he completed the Mountain Climbing Instructors Course in Alaska and language school, in Chinese Mandarin. During this three-year period he also participated in several TDY (Temporary Duty Assignment) tours in Laos and Vietnam.

CHAPTER 7
PIONEER SURGEONS

Throughout the process of developing and implementing medical training standards, not enough can be said about the surgeons. They provided the basis on which the medics learned their highly sophisticated skills. Carey Drumheller, while stationed in Germany, again points to his training with Colonel Shrum and Major Gilpatrick, "I admired the colonel and the major, both were professional Army. I went to clinic with them, pre-op, operating room, and post-op. I was often asked what my opinion was on a particular diagnosis. This of course was flattering to a Staff Sergeant. I know they were testing me and they were teaching me a hell of a lot."[76] The training privileges created friction with traditional military personnel. This was not always the case, but it would be a constant theme that all medics in training would encounter and have to overcome. In hindsight, that friction also provided a valuable lesson. It presented the medic with the opportunity to overcome unforeseen challenges and to accomplish a task that would serve them well in the future. The ability to not become frustrated and hindered could mean the difference between life and death.

Another Medical Corps (MC) officer who contributed immensely in the early development of the SF medics is Colonel Valentine B. Sky (Ret.). Colonel Sky had his first exposure to Special Forces in late 1954. He was in charge of the 119th Medical Detachment in Bad Tölz Germany, providing medical services to the dependents of military members. Dr. Sky recalled his first impressions of the new unit [Special Forces].

> "They had their own doctor, an MSC officer, and I had an opportunity to see how the Special Forces operated. Right after I was in the 5th Engineer Combat Battalion, which was stationed in Giessen, and I had seen just one year of American way of life in the service. My experience with Special Forces in Bad Tölz at that time showed quite a different picture from conventional units. I was very much impressed by their activities and their attitude of soldiering. I believe this exposure to Special Forces contaminated me and then in 1959 after I finished the advanced course at Fort Sam Houston, I asked for assignment to Special Forces."[77]

Many of the early doctors and surgeons should be especially noted for their work and dedication to the furtherance of medicine in Special Forces. An assignment to Special Forces was virtually considered career stopping. Special Forces, for the most part, were not highly thought of within US Army command elements, especially by officers who wished to advance in rank. Colonel Sky's comments about his own request to transfer to Special Forces reflect those feelings among the regular Army officers.

> "My request at that time was considered unfavorable and I was sent back to 101st Airborne Division in Fort Campbell, Kentucky. In Fort Campbell, I was Battalion Surgeon of the 626th Engineering Battalion, Airborne. Then with the Medical Company, then with the Division Artillery, and finally I became acting Division Surgeon in 1959. In December 1959, I said goodbye to General Westmoreland, who used to be at that time, the Division Commander, and I took my family, three kids, my wife and a dog, and took off for Okinawa."[78]

Colonel Sky, at the time a Major, arrived on Okinawa to join the 1st Special Forces Group February 22, 1960. "That was my most colorful and pleasant assignment in military career."[79] He describes with joy his time and happy memories and on a personal level that is endemic to all Special Forces members. "My family enjoyed very much Okinawa, and my wife enjoyed that she was taken in, in a very nice circle of ladies from the 1st Special Forces Group, and we felt we belonged to one little family. I spent three and a half years in Okinawa."[80] It is indeed a very special family.

CHAPTER 8
BELIEF IN MISSION

The early day medics deserve a great deal of recognition for their dedication and perseverance in their profession and mission. Many of the first medics were left to their own devices to gain further information concerning medical operational matters. No clear precedent for the SF medical support existed and the few historical records remaining from OSS operations during World War II left little in the way of a 'blueprint' for the medics. Al Maggio recalls;

> "Most of us would read about the exploits of the OSS, partisan unit accomplishments in Europe and Asia. But, this informational reading list was very short on medical intelligence that we needed badly and many records were destroyed after WW II. One book *Guerrilla Surgeon* by Captain Lindsay Rogers, a British Medical Officer that went into Yugoslavia during WW II, was the best I could find to get information for insight of what could be before us. He explained the constant problem of the effects of un-evacuated casualties, the bad methods of amputation and wound debridements. Along with these problems were supply and re-supply systems that did not work and the setting up of guerrilla hospitals in the mountainous areas. This, I found, would be my 'bible' of guidance for the following years until we developed a Standard Operating Procedure (SOP) for medical support in any given theater, to address these problems for medical support in the unconventional warfare setting. Mission success depended upon the units being

> allocated proper support in the operational zone in which they operated."[81]

Al Maggio played a unique role in the early development of Special Forces by being on the ground floor of many 'firsts' in SF history. From 1952 to 1957 he was a part of the formation of four separate Groups (10th, 77th, 1st as well as the 8231st Special Operations Detachment). As a testament to how dedicated and seriously the medics took their jobs, the following defines the lengths to which the medics would go to obtain the best possible training. During this time Maggio left Special Forces for a year to attend the Walter Reed Hospital's Clinical Specialist Course. He explained that in his case,

> "I knew I was going to make it a career. I just wanted to be sure I knew what the hell I was doing. We were going to be in a guerrilla situation where you would have to have a hidden cache of wounded to care for. I got a lot out of that course."[82]

The completion of that intensified training provided him with an LPN license (Licensed Practical Nurse) and more importantly, he took that knowledge and skill back to Special Forces to share and help train future medics, as part of the training cadre at Ft. Bragg. The initiative displayed by Maggio was common among medics in their desire to learn and upgrade their skills.

1954 through 1957, were very busy years for the expansion of Special Forces. After the 10th Group departed for Germany, the newly formed 77th Group at Ft. Bragg continued to build up its strength. In June of 1956, three officers and thirteen NCO's were hand picked to form the 14th SFOF (Special Forces Operational Detachment). This unit was sent to Hawaii, as a control team, in preparation for missions in Thailand, Taiwan and Vietnam. Two of the members, Chalmers Archer Jr. and Lester Ruper, were the Detachment medics. Soon thereafter, the 8231st Special Operations Detachment was formed and based at Camp Drake, Japan. Among the medics were Earle Peckham and Al Maggio. The team composed of five officers and seventeen NCO's, conducted training operations in the Asian theater. They provided training for foreign Ranger and Special Forces, such as the Thai Special Forces (the old Royal Thai Rangers).

Paul Campbell recalls, "The Thailand trips were sometime around 1957 through 1960. They were only for short trips of thirty days or less."[83] These missions revolved around training and area studies without plans for civic action or medical programs. Campbell recalls,

> "On one mission when we were training with the Thai Border Patrol, we jumped into an area in the northwest section of the county above Chieng Mai. On another mission we did area studies along the Laos and Cambodian borders, working out of Udorn on this trip. Medical treatment was limited to our team members and some villages that we came across, but these missions were devoted to other [things] than rendering medical treatments. The Thai Border Patrol was a sort of police military unit and they were airborne qualified. They got training in patrolling, ambushes, operations and we got a look at the land and terrain and of course the people."[84]

Campbell also recalled that the medics' skills were also employed during Special Forces training missions and field exercises. There was always a medic assigned to routine duties, such as jump zone coverage.

> "When we were assigned to cover a jump we would go with an ambulance and driver to the Drop Zone (DZ) and treat any injuries on the ground and transport them to the hospital. Jumping is a safe sport but…they jump a lot at night and in many drop zones that are very small, so people do get hurt, and people have been killed. I've covered a lot of jumps as a medic and seen some bad injuries. A good teammate got killed as one of the first SF Free Fallers HALO [High Altitude Low Opening] concept being trained back in the early 60's."[85]

Unfortunately, accidents are a part of military operations. One such occasion occurred in March of 1954. A C-119 'flying boxcar' crashed into the 77th Group's Mess Hall at Ft. Bragg. Al Maggio vividly recalls that horrible day.

> "It happened at five after ten in the morning. I was across the street in the supply room and heard a whining motor so I looked outside and up over Reilly Road this plane was headed south but was turning to come north to head into the airfield. He never made it. It hit a chimney on the Headquarters building of the 77th Group, landed in the parade field and slid into the mess hall. We had just got out of there at coffee call, so hundreds of guys had just got out of there, it was amazing how this happened. So, I ran across the street and warned everyone to stay away because there might be an explosion, there wasn't a fire yet. I heard screaming and moaning coming from the crash site. A bunch of us ran into the mess hall area where the plane was sticking out. The whole nose was sticking out on the street. The rest of the building was resting on top of the plane itself and the two engines were covered partly. One side blew up; the left side gas tanks blew up, a lot of flames and fire going on. That was the side where the door was for the pilot and co pilot to climb in and out. I couldn't get inside the building because that's where most of them died inside there, got burned up. It was terrible. A lot of them jumped out coming down, hitting telephone poles and got killed. A lot of the men in the plane got killed jumping out of the damn thing when it was coming in fast, it was so sad. I got inside with another fella, Gene Hunt. We got into the pilots' compartment and got them both out slowly, their arms were hanging and their legs were all tore up from the metal. It was terrible. I looked down and there was this hat, the co pilot had his name inside it. His name was Alexander; I'll never forget it to this day. We got them both to the hospital in a Group ambulance and then came back. We couldn't get anymore bodies out. There was nothing lying there. We had two KP's killed in the building—Greenleaf

> and I cant remember the other one now. We had a cook who had his leg cut off. These were the casualties from Group—the Air Force had others beside the pilot and co pilot. We stayed there till six that night helping. The other wing didn't blow. The right side didn't blow. Thank God, it would've been even worse, Oh my God. They drained 800 gallons of fuel from it the next day. Five or six of us got the Soldier's Medal[86] for helping out and evacuating the wounded. Fred Williamson, Tony Buchear and Gene Hunt are the names I can remember. You didn't know till later who all was helping.[87] You never looked around to see who is helping; you grabbed and did what you could. Guys were chopping on the roof and going through trying to get inside to where the plane was, a lot of guys stuck their neck out doing dangerous things."[88]

Maggio remembers the ceremony on the parade field for awarding the Soldiers Medal, "they carried it on a pillow and the Colonel pinned it on my chest", he said with a nervous almost shy giggle, "it was unbelievable."[89]

Drumheller recalled another training accident that required him to react to a medical emergency while with the 10th Group in Germany. He wasn't assigned to DZ coverage for this particular accident and isn't sure who attended the injured man initially in the field, but was involved with his treatment at the 2nd Field Hospital in Munich. In his own words "this is not a pretty story", but is very descriptive and indicative of the type of situation that the medic would or could encounter and must be prepared to care for and treat.

> "The jump was a night jump in very poor weather. Light rain and mist, low clouds and cold, but not freezing. I think it was probably in the early fall of 1954. I was working at the 2nd Field Hospital in Munich. I needed a jump for pay purposes.[90] A couple of FA teams [forerunner of today's 'A' Detachment] were to make a night jump into an area and play 'Sneaky Pete' for a few weeks. The drop zone had been selected by some-

one and arrangements made with the Germans to use their pasture. The Germans were to turn of the power on a line along the road parallel to the DZ. I had just tagged along; smug in the knowledge that I would be sleeping warm and dry and not in a wet damn sleeping bag. Everyone figured that we would not jump because of the weather. We would occasionally see clouds BELOW us. Wrong! There was a hole and the green light came on—we jumped. This is where the fun started. The DZ had been fertilized with the 'honey wagon' that day, wet, slick and whew! I was on the ground and saw some sparks from the direction of the power line. We knew it was there because that had been covered in the pre-jump briefing, but considered it not a real hazard. This was a mistake because some light wind had come up and some of the men barely missed the line (did not know it until their chute draped over it when they hit the ground). The man in question must have hit the ground wire and hot wire also because his clothes caught on fire. I remember riding an ambulance back to the hospital in Munich, but for the life of me I do not remember if it was in the ambulance transporting him.

Over the next few days, probably a couple of weeks, I assisted in helping dress his burns. He was hospitalized in an individual room on a rubber sheet with a makeshift tent over him. Everything close to him was sterile and the room super clean. We wore scrubs and masks when we entered the room. I think it was about every couple days that he would go to surgery and we would literally wash off dead skin. There was a square patch of flesh on his back about 12 x 18 inches where the parachute backpack had been pressing. This was not burned. His head was not burned because he had a pile cap and helmet on. There were no burns on his feet or ankles because of his boots. After he was given the anesthesia, we would sit him up by hanging on to his hair (he did not have a crew cut) and outstretching his arms by grabbing his hands. The Doctor's

> would then proceed to dress his burns. He had burns from both the clothing and the electricity. He was later sent to the States, where I assume they started grafting when he healed up."[91]

With the rapid expansion and changes in Special Forces during the final years of the 1950's, came more strains on the medical training for the different Groups now spread across the globe. The training procedures became more standardized in the United States and in Germany, each with their unique advantages. However, the newly formed 1st Special Forces Group on Okinawa would undergo some growing pains in developing its training and support structure.

CHAPTER 9

INTO ASIA

In June of 1957 the 14th and 8231st combined to form the nucleus for the 1st Special Forces Group. The new Group was now responsible for Far Eastern Operations and training missions with counterparts in Korea, South Vietnam, Taiwan and the Philippines. The 1st Group 'set up shop' on the island of Okinawa; since…"the Japanese Peace Treaty of '53 precluded the open recognition of unconventional warfare activities in Japan."[92]

At this time there was no Medical Officer to oversee the medical needs and training assigned to the Psychological Warfare Center at Ft. Bragg. The only consistency in training was what the medics received at Ft. Sam Houston. It was left up to the individual Group Surgeons to prescribe the medical training for their units. At the 1st Group's activation there was no provision in the TO&E (Table of Organization and Equipment) for a Surgeon. Initially, there was an Medical Service Corps Captain, Sigurd Bue, but his duties were mainly non-medical, as he was assigned to be the Group intelligence officer. Senior medics were utilized to conduct Group medical training and the proficiency programs. This was born of necessity, rather than design, because of the manpower shortage due to post-Korean War cutbacks. Captain Bue does recall that he conducted some classes, "it might be a First Aid class today. It could be a dental class tomorrow…I didn't personally put together and ramrod any medic training program."[93] His role as Group Surgeon, according to Bue "was almost non functional. My role there was primarily intelligence."[94]

Colonel Sky, the first 1st Group Surgeon, also recalls that there wasn't much of a Medical Detachment upon his arrival. The first medical NCOIC, Sergeant Troy Dillinder, deployed to Vietnam soon after Sergeant Edward Montgomery arrived on Okinawa as 1959 was ending. With the arrival of Colonel Sky the 1st Group medical program grew at a very rapid pace. Colonel Sky took an immediate liking to his new unit and NCOIC.

> "…There in the Medical Detachment, as such, or dispensary, as such, were only Major Sky, the doctor, and Sergeant Montgomery, NCOIC, medic, supply man, everything you can imagine…My biggest helper was Ed Montgomery…when I walked in, he just jumped up on his feet and said, 'I'm glad to see you Major Sky; now, at least we have a doctor.'…I came from conventional outfit, and the way Special Forces operated, unconventionally, it was a new trick to me, which I picked up from him very fast."[95]

Colonel Sky set out to provide the necessary training and practice procedures that he had witnessed back in Bad Tölz Germany. In conjunction with his counterpart at Camp Kue Hospital, Colonel Roger Juel, MC, an OJT program was established. The medics could now obtain training in orthopedic and surgical procedures as well as general medicine and emergency room practices. Colonel Juel recalled that;

> "The first time that training became more formalized was when Sky joined us. He was with us constantly. He worked on the training of these people. It was a pretty small outfit though, and was not possible to train great numbers. A lot of them were out on deployment and such activities at that time. We never saw more than three or four students at a time."[96]

Okinawa buzzed with activity to establish logistical and supply support for missions in the new area of responsibility. In January 1959 Montgomery was tasked with developing a load listing for supplies initially taken with a deploying team, for six months, for a mission involving twelve A Teams in an Asiatic country. He would not find out until May that the teams were for the HOTFOOT Program in Laos. A system had to be developed to account for the available equipment and supply inventory of approximately 130 items. A numbering system was applied for coding purposes. This was accomplished through a breakdown of the basic drugs and medications, their stock number, quantities available, the drugs use and dosage. This information was then compiled, then coded for radio transmission for ordering purposes. The project took about four months to complete.

An interesting sidelight to this was that there was only about $10,000 to supply the outbound detachments. This posed a slight problem, in that, Montgomery felt that each team should take $1,000 worth of surgical soap with them. Soap was not only used as a barter item in Asia, but each person who sought treatment would be required to thoroughly wash, before treatment was given. This turned out to be a pretty successful training program, Montgomery recalls, the "majority of patients were sadly lacking soap."[97] A psychological benefit was also added to the program by having either a handshake or a flag of the country stamped on each bar of soap.

Meeting the needs of deployed teams, as well as budgetary constraints, created unique situations that required creative fast thinking, in one such instance, 'Monty' recognized a need for a scarce medication. He recalls 'inventing' a cheaper, but equally effective common vitamin.

> "We had a vast demand for vitamin tablets. Doc Sky and I talked it over, he said, 'Well, you know we can get yeast tablets and yeast tablets are much cheaper than regular multiple vitamin tablets. They have a certain amount of B Complex in them, plus a bunch of other vitamins. Why don't we order those and repackage them and send them out as multiple vitamins?' I told him we can't very well put yeast tablets on there [supply sheet] because nobody will order them. So, he said, 'Give them a fancy name.' I was sitting there packaging them with a

> man named Williams. We looked at one another and said we will call it WAM, 'W' out of Williams, 'A' out of And, and 'M' out of Montgomery. We just sent these WAM vitamin tablets down into Laos and Vietnam."[98]

Dr. Sky's influence significantly enhanced the 1st Group's medical training and the skills that would be required for the medics to perform the Special Forces mission.

The local indigenous tribes throughout the Okinawa area presented an ideal situation to practice the Special Forces need to develop a relationship with the local people in the area of deployment. Medical assistance programs were established in the villages around Okinawa and it's surrounding small islands. Dr. Sky and two or three medics took footlockers full of medical supplies and went to the schools and conducted physicals for the children and then treated the local adult population. One village in particular had been 'adopted' by the 1st Group Medical Detachment, after Montgomery and Sky formulated the idea to make one of the local villages a model project. This model was eventually duplicated in many villages in Vietnam.

The village of Sosu and its people loved the medical treatment and reinforced the model that Special Forces developed, Dr. Sky tells of an officer becoming lost during a parachute training exercise and landing in Sosu village. Upon recognizing the man's Green Beret and learning that he was a friend with Sr. Sora (Dr. Sky in Japanese), he was taken in by the villagers, fed and housed for the night. The officer would later tell Dr. Sky, "Val, I was really treated like royalty in Sosu village…"[99], attesting to the fact that the medical treatment received by indigenous people could win their support. "That proves that the Special Forces medic can make friends anyplace he goes. And we need the friends and particularly in foreign countries. Without help from the natives we would be lost anyplace. And how can you make a friend better than removing his miseries and problems."[100] Indeed, Colonel Sky summed up the importance of this part of the Special Forces medical mission.

Conducting medical aid programs for the indigenous people was of far more value than any amount of foreign aid to a guerrilla force.

Many of the medics who served in Laos with the Hotfoot Teams during 1959, later the White Star Mobile Training Teams (WSMTT), and the first teams that operated in South Vietnam, came from the 1st Group, via TDY assignments. Chalmers Archer Jr. served as an original member of the 14th SFOD, in Hawaii in 1956 and later the 1st Special Forces Group. The 14th SFOD was selected to go into Vietnam and establish a training program for a Vietnamese counterpart Special Forces unit. The 14th was well versed in this type of mission, as they had previously performed the same missions in Thailand and Taiwan.

By all accounts available, Archer and SFC Lester G. Ruper, were the first Special Forces medics in South Vietnam. The team arrived June 21, 1957 and set up an intensive training program, modeled on the specialty skills of an A Detachment. Archer recalls the medical training portion of the mission and how they "tried to copy what Ft. Sam Houston did, within our limitations. Teach everything we were taught…although we did not have the facilities. I set up a hospital building in Nha Trang (ward training) and tried to do exactly what was done within practical means."[101] Given the circumstances, Archer felt that the program was very successful.

Tragically, there was a high price paid with the first foray into Vietnam. Until now, questions surrounded the mortal wounding of Captain Harry G. Cramer and SFC Ruper's loss of an arm. The initial investigation report from the Department of the Army indicated that a block of TNT exploded in the hands of an indigenous trainee, causing massive fatal head injuries to Captain Cramer. That is not what actually happened. Archer recounts the events of that day in his book *Green Berets in the Vanguard.* Archer recalls, several hours after midnight on October 21, 1957 the men of the 14th SFOD left the city of Nha Trang with their new class of Vietnamese trainees for a graduation ceremony to celebrate their recent completion of the course.

On the morning of the 21st, two suspected NVA soldiers had been captured, an interrogation conducted by Captain Cramer confirmed what they already suspected. An attempt on their lives was to be made in the near future. The team felt quite vulnerable in the ominous landscape of towering mountains and thick jungles of Vietnam, where danger could be found everywhere. Nevertheless, they continued with their plans and implemented higher security precautions.

Around three in the afternoon, enemy mortar fire struck the graduation field with devastating effect. Captain Cramer suffered serious head wounds and SFC Ruper had had his hand blown off. Archer, with the help of VNSF (Vietnamese Special Forces) personnel loaded Cramer and Ruper onto the back of a 'deuce and one half' (two and one half ton utility truck). Archer best describes the mind-numbing brutality of war.

> "After checking again to make sure that Sergeant Ruper's tourniquet remained secure, I turned my attention back to Captain Cramer. He was unconscious, but his body still moved spastically, as if he were attempting to sit up. Although I knew it would have taken a miracle for Captain Cramer to survive his wounds, I wanted to reassure myself that I was doing all I could to save his life. I unfastened the chinstrap of his helmet. From the nature of the flow of blood, I knew the main wound was probably under his right armpit. As I tried hard to bandage it, I sensed that my efforts were in vain. In a matter of seconds, he was dead. I could not speak; my lips were moving, but no sound came out."[102]

Archer is unsure, to this day, where the attackers came from. It was swift, harsh, well planned and executed at the most unexpected time. The 30-caliber rifle fire, mortars, rapid succession of grenade explosions punctuated with small arms fire had caught the group by complete surprise. Archer is reasonably sure that people from the local village and possibly even members of the newly trained Vietnamese Special Forces troops took part in the attack.

Was this an omen for the impending conflict in Vietnam? It is without question a vivid example of the danger the men of Special Forces faced—losing not only a patient, but also a friend, a person with whom you trained and lived. "He died in my arms, he was the last person I took care of. It took an awful long time…half of his head was gone."[103] These events left an indelible mark on Archer's life.

> "In the early hours of 22 October 1957, I boarded a plane provided by General Samuel Williams, commanding general of the United States, MAAG, Vietnam, and escorted Sergeant Ruper and Captain Cramer's body to the Philippines, where I remained for a couple of weeks. The attack occurred on the last official training date for that particular mission."[104]

Captain Harry G. Cramer was the first American casualty of the Vietnam War. His name was finally etched in the black stone of the Vietnam Veterans Memorial in Washington D.C. on November 11, 1983—thanks, in part, to the efforts of Archer's lasting devotion.

Medics like Paul Campbell who helped establish the 1st Special Forces Group Medical Detachment, realized the positive results from their early struggles to establish a training and support structure. Campbell felt he was lucky in many ways, "because I'd been in Okie (Okinawa) almost four years prior to going to Nam. Colonel Sky, the first Group Surgeon, and his NCOIC, Montgomery, believed in hands on training for us, so we got a lot of treatment training in our field trips in and out of Okie."[105] At the time, although he wasn't aware of it, Campbell was gaining valuable experience that would serve him well in establishing what would become a significant part of Special Forces operations in the Republic of Vietnam.

Montgomery's arrival in June 1959 brought some much-needed organization to the medical detachment. For example, he and six other medics inventoried every item in the warehouse. They soon found things that they could never use. "We had complete operating tables, lamps and material packaged in sterile packers for about three or four years. We determined what could be used and the rest was returned for creditable return to the US Army Camp Kue Hospital."[106] Research by the medics of the 1st Special Forces Group, before arrival of a Group Surgeon, gave birth to the handbook of prevalent diseases, their signs, symptoms and cures. It was later reproduced (with some minor changes) for the 5th Special Forces Group when it was activated and deployed to Vietnam in 1964. During the latter part of 1959 the medics in Okinawa sat down and divided, on a map, the areas between Antarctica, the Continental limits of the US and the border of Western Europe. This may sound like an enormous task but, according to MSG Montgomery, "fortunately, disease knows no borders."[107] Each medic was then assigned countries within a geographical area to develop an area study. Next, the prevalent diseases in the area had a "brief outline written with its signs, symptoms and drug of choice for treatment of the diseases."[108] The booklet "was written in lay language so any team member could look it up, read it and come up with a differential diagnosis and treat accordingly."[109]

By 1960, survey teams went into countries such as, Taiwan, Korea, Philippines, Vietnam and Indonesia. To support these rapidly growing hot spots the 1st Groups medical budget grew from $39,000 in 1958 to over $250,000 in 1962. A system emerged for recording and tracking diseases, illnesses and injuries the medics had treated. A Patient Treatment Record was kept by the medics, in which they would denote, using hash marks, treatments corresponding to a particular category. This system provided the source data for monthly reports maintained by the C Team and served as a perpetual inventory mechanism. By compiling and calculating the various maladies and the supplies necessary to treat them, the quantity of medicine and other expendable supplies could be determined with better accuracy, enabling the supply channels to maintain proper stock levels of these items closer to the operational team and reduce resupply time.

CHAPTER 10

FULL CIRCLE, BACK TO BRAGG

As the 1st Group worked out the logistics for their medical program, back at Ft. Bragg, the 77th Group was developing a five week surgical training course to be taught at Ft. Bragg, at the Advanced Medical Training School (AMTS). Over the years, the name of this facility would change from Surgical Research Laboratory to Clinical Research Laboratory to Advanced Medical Research Lab and finally, today's Joint Special Operations Medical Training Center (JSOMTC). The course taught at this facility initially lasted five weeks, and was extended to eight weeks in the early 1960's. SFC Ralph Drouin, the first NCOIC of the facility recalled the uncertain and unstructured training regimen, "The initial training was more or less played by ear…we tried different procedures to see how well the enlisted men would pick up on these procedures. See how much they could handle and just what we could give them."[110] SFC Drouin, possessed impressive medical training requisites that included being a graduate of the Naval Hospital Corps School, Independent School for Medical Corpsmen, Dental Technician School, Para-rescue and Survival School and the Medical Specialist Advanced Course at Fitzsimmons General Hospital.[111] Drouin also possessed another equally important ability to 'locate' needed medical supplies and equipment, which is a signature of all Special Forces soldiers. It would not be the last time the quick thinking ability to 'acquire' needed materials to accomplish a task would be demonstrated by a resourceful medic.

In the summer of 1959 Captain John L. Bond, MC, received approval to establish a small surgical research facility in the 'old hospital' area across Ardennes Road from Womack Army Hospital. Captain Bond wanted to provide additional surgical practice for hospital surgeons. An informal agreement between Captain Bond and the 77th Group Surgeon provided the manpower from the 77th Group to maintain the facility. In return, hospital physicians and SF medics had the opportunity for hands on training. Drouin recalls that it was September of 1959 when the first class of four medics began the "initial start of the regular Advanced Medical Training School."[112] From this humble beginning, it became the framework for the toughest phases of all the medical training for every medic who graduated. It is here, that the medic was put to the ultimate test of everything he had learned up to this point. Classes consisted of varying numbers of men depending upon how many people could be spared from the Group. E. Grant Madison also involved with the initial organization of the facility, recalled, "The organization was, 'lets just pull four medics over this week and train for a little bit.' It was really not like a school. There were not any specific numbers designated initially, it was people from Group training people from Group."[113] The philosophy of training from the beginning was, as Madison explained, "Working where you were isolated completely, without a physician. With no evacuation, and be able to do just about what anyone could do under combat conditions; under *combat conditions!*"[114]

Al Maggio attended AMTS when he returned to Ft. Bragg from Okinawa in March 1959. He recalled how the AMTS evolved to become an integral part of the training.

> "The location for the training was ideal in that the old hospital area was available to use, as the new Womack Army Hospital was completed and left the old operating room and adjacent buildings intact for the Group Surgeon to start this badly needed phase of training to support the UW medical

effort in a more professional manner. Good diplomacy was again applied here and with the SWC [Special Warfare Center] Surgeon and Group Surgeon efforts presented a POI [Program of Instruction[115]] that the XVIII Airborne Corps and Womack Army Hospital Surgeons and the training officers went along with the plan. It utilized most of the OR [operating room] equipment that was not transferred to the new hospital site. The POI consisted of Diagnostics and Treatment classes, Drug Therapy and Surgeon, Nurse and Anesthetist techniques used in the OR. Instrument nomenclature and use of specific instruments for wound debridement and venous cut-down to include amputation were taught. Movies were shown on the latest methods of sterilization, incision, wound debridement and amputation during classroom instruction. Use of blood volume expanders were taught to prevent shock and to maintain patient stability, along with classes on the stages of anesthesia. We had available Ether and Sodium Pentathol for anesthetic use, plus Pontacaine and Lidocaine for local or dental use if required. The drop method for ether was taught. After completing the classroom phase, each man was assigned a patient."[116]

In less than six months, the Program of Instruction for the Advanced Medical Training School was essentially formalized. The medics functioned as an operating room team, Surgeon, Scrub Nurse and Anesthetist, in a rotation that placed the medic as Surgeon when his 'patient' was having the operation performed. The 'patient' was treated for a Russian 7.62 carbine wound from start to finish. The medics assessed the damage, applied the initial battle dressing and once the 'patient' was in the operating room and IV (intravenous tube) was administered and an airway established by means of inserting an intra-tracheal tube. The wound would require debridement and amputation. Maggio also noted the emphasis placed on "keeping progression records, meds (medicines) ordered or stopped, nursing notes on procedures taken and OR forms were required throughout the phase."[117] This is most often where the reality of what they had been learning sunk in and it was very sobering. The academic struggles at Ft. Sam Houston paled in comparison to the intensity level encountered at the AMTS. This final phase was the most difficult and produced the attrition rates. It was and still is the ultimate test of their skill and desire.

The AMTS was unique in its advanced curriculum for enlisted personnel with the instruction provided by senior enlisted medics. Many of the medics remember their instructor(s) from this phase. When asked if whether an enlisted medic taught this course made a difference, the answer was invariably, "yes!" Maggio recalled how, "The instructor positioned himself to give constructive criticism and kept records of each man's procedures and critiqued the men as an "OR Team' and separately as required."[118] That the instructor had gone through the same training and been assigned to operational detachments and had put the training to use in practical situations held a lot of weight with the trainees. The instructor was someone who had practiced what he was teaching.

Al Maggio recalls his instructor even after all these years, "MSG Gregory Matteo. Great guy, what a wonderful guy. Every year or two the instructors would change, with the guys rotating back from Laos and Vietnam. The curriculum was constantly upgraded."[119] This rotation provided trainees with the latest developments in actual operational settings. Once again, there were no steadfast rules for this training. However, this began to change rapidly with reports coming back from medics who had recently served in Laos, showing a clear need for more advanced medical training. "We gained a lot of experience from medics coming back from Vietnam and Laos who were wounded. We would get them as instructors…and they could relate all their experiences and what they went through."[120] Madison recalls one former instructor, SSG Billy Hall, who exemplifies the commitment and dedication the medics possessed and the heroic acts that inspired all. During the March 9, 1966 attack of Camp A 102, Ashau, while attending wounded, an incoming mortar round severed SSG Hall's legs. Hall put tourniquets on both of his legs and continued to administer aid until he couldn't crawl anymore.[121]

The availability of official documentation creates a conundrum when attempting to affix a specific date for the first time that Special Forces medical training clearly defined specific criteria for all medical personnel training prior to assignment to an 'A' Detachment. The following, extracted from a brief summary by the Special Forces Medical Division at Ft. Bragg, outlining the training program in place during 1959 represents the earliest known formalized training requirements.[122]

> "The training undergone by an individual which qualifies him as a Special Forces Medic is among the longest and most intensive in the Army. His entire medical training requires 32 weeks of instruction conducted by physicians, nurses, and the best Non-Commissioned Officer instructors in the army, who, themselves are experienced Special Forces Medics. The 32 weeks are divided into several phases:
>
> 1. Special Forces Basic Aidman's Course—Conducted at Fort Bragg, N.C. Prepares the student to understand the principles of the medicine and nursing. 8 weeks in length.
> 2. 300 F-1 Course (Mos 91B)—at Fort Sam Houston, Texas. Introduces the student to diagnosis and treatment of diseases and prepares him to perform the important manual medical techniques he will need. 10 weeks in length.
> 3. OJT—On the Job Training conducted at a number of Army Hospitals. The student will function as an extern under the guidance of the hospital staff in various sections of the hospital. 7 weeks in length.
> 4. AMTS—Advanced Medical Training School, conducted at Fort Bragg, N.C. Is divided into 2 Phases:
>   a. Advanced Medical Lectures: 3 weeks.
>   b. Advanced Surgical Laboratory: 4 weeks.
>
> Total of 7 weeks in length

> Contained within this brief[123] is a more extensive breakdown of the material contained within each of these courses of instruction. The student is continually examined both orally and on written examinations. The requirement for acceptance into the course is among the Army's most stringent and the attrition rate is high. Prior to graduation each student is examined orally by a board of physicians and senior medics, who will permit no one but those qualified to graduate."[124]

As the tumultuous 1950's drew to a close, Communist expansion by means of subversion and guerrilla warfare found Special Forces in a prime position to play a major role. Unseen and unknown at the time, Special Forces was in places that most Americans had never even heard about, or knew that there was a war taking place. Laos was one of those countries. It was here that SF received an introduction to counter-insurgency tactics and warfare. In July of 1959, the first teams arrived, 'in the black', in Vientiane, the capital of Laos. Air America, the civilian airline operated by the CIA, ferried the teams and their supplies and provided additional air support. The Laotian experience could be considered the 'dress rehearsal' for Vietnam.

From a medical standpoint, much information was developed through trial and error as information was sent back to Ft. Bragg from these distant locales. Training would be changed or added and updated. Information regarding tropical diseases was sketchy at best. Deployed teams, especially in Laos, changed that. This was due to the lack of intimate knowledge in Southeast Asia. It was virtually unknown territory. The people, their customs and the multiple dialects, which were spoken within the same country among the myriad of ethnic entities. The land itself was not well known and mostly unmapped. The plants, the animals and the weather were unfamiliar. There was no systematic procedure in place to collect and transmit medical intelligence. Causing many difficulties for replacement teams that rotated every six months. They relied on their ability to function in the unknown and learning by doing. The Special Forces teams that operated in the program, known as 'HOTFOOT' and later 'WHITE STAR', would extract and use the information amazingly well.

Special Forces medical experiences in Laos were not well documented. Captain Samuel Skemp, MC, who accompanied the first Special Forces teams into Laos, felt that the teams were as well prepared medically as could be expected, given the limited knowledge about tropical diseases. They conducted pre-mission training consisting of film reviews and technical manuals. Additionally, some of the medics had gone through OJT at VA Hospitals, for 12 to 18 months, acquiring the skills, perhaps, equivalent to that of a Registered Nurse. Skemp concedes, "That may be a little bit of an exaggeration, but they were well trained, no question about it, comparatively."[125]

The team's primary mission was to train members of the Royal Lao Army. The medical training mission for 'HOTFOOT' was to train the Royal Lao Army medics. During this period there was to be little treatment provided to the indigenous population. The training plan for the Lao medics mirrored that of the SF medics. How much was actually taught them would depend on how well the Laotians absorbed the basic first aid instruction. The effectiveness of that training is not clear since, to varying degrees, language difficulties hampered each individual team medic. Dr. Skemp felt that the language barrier might have been the biggest problem of the operation. The interpreters were not able to communicate to all the Lao medics due to the different dialects that changed from province to province and sometimes from village to village. However, this was the first rotation of teams and as of yet there was little information exchanged between outbound and inbound teams and information filtered back to the Group Headquarters in Ft. Bragg.[126]

The C Team Headquarters was set up in Vientiane and the Surgeon, Dr. Skemp, was stationed there to provide any support that the medics needed. Stationed at training centers, the medics, for the most part, had no direct supervision from a doctor. They didn't encounter a lot of medical problems, except with the water, which could cause diarrhea and other intestinal maladies if not properly chlorinated. As U.S. involvement in the region grew, the unsupervised environment in which the medics operated concerned some U.S. Surgeon's. This concern concentrated around the medics' abilities to diagnose and treat in some instances put them in a position over their heads. Dr. Skemp shared his thoughts about this:

> "Well, this could be, but how the heck you gonna say for sure. You know, in any form of treatment, first of all, you've got to make the right diagnosis. Well Christ, this day and age…well, you know, a diagnosis often entails, at least to really do it right, a certain amount of sophisticated lab work which nobody had anyway. I don't know. I…sure, maybe theoretically they did go a little overboard, but I guess my feeling is that the odds were they were more often than not, doing more good than harm. Or at least doing no harm if they treated a fever with an antibiotic that possibly was a virus disease…that's going to happen once in awhile. So I don't know under the circumstances how that could have been improved upon."[127]

Dr. Skemp's observation and opinion reflects what the medic was taught and the creed to "Do No Harm".

The early experiences in Laos and Vietnam brought change to the training procedures. Better diagnostic courses were developed and implemented at Ft. Sam. Standardized requirements were developed for written reports of medical activities. Then, this information was disseminated for future training and deployment considerations.

Medics operating in the field without direct supervision had positive and negative experiences. Positive because they were capable of operating and handling situations in a real environment. Negative because of the lack of coordinated communication with the Surgeons assigned to Vientiane and with the individual medics scattered throughout the country. Special Forces was moving rapidly into a new role based on political decisions by the Soviets to expand communism's reach through insurgent activities. The United States was committed to countering that expansion. Special Forces would perform with unyielding dedication and honor.

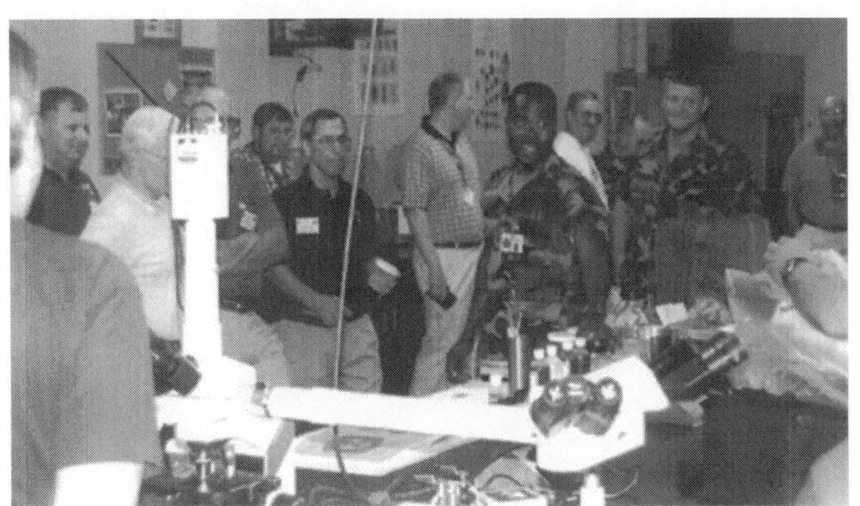

Figure 1

Figure 2

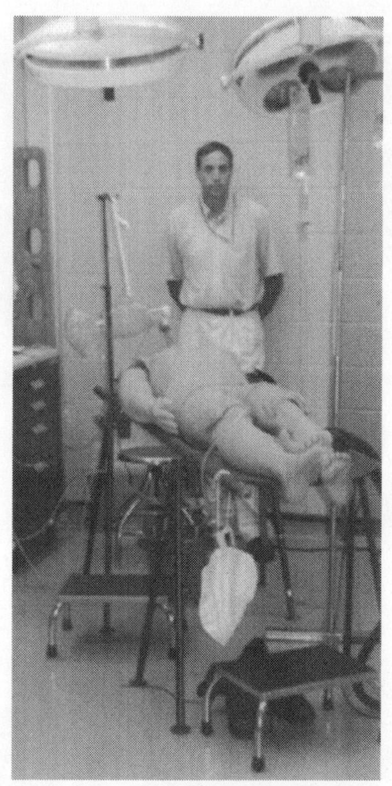

Figure 3

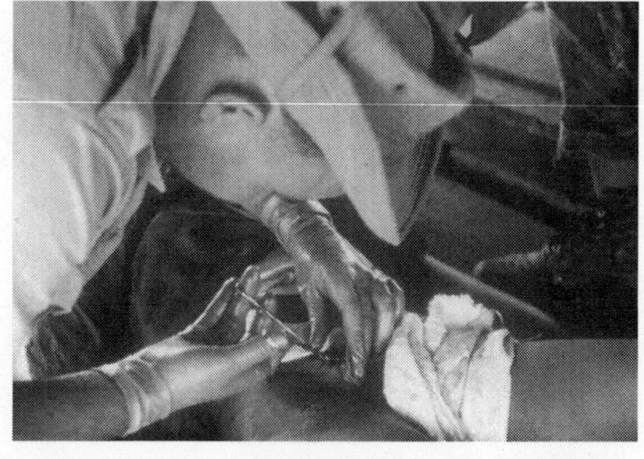

Figure 4

Figure 5

Figure 6

Figure 7

Figure 8

Figure 9

Figure 10

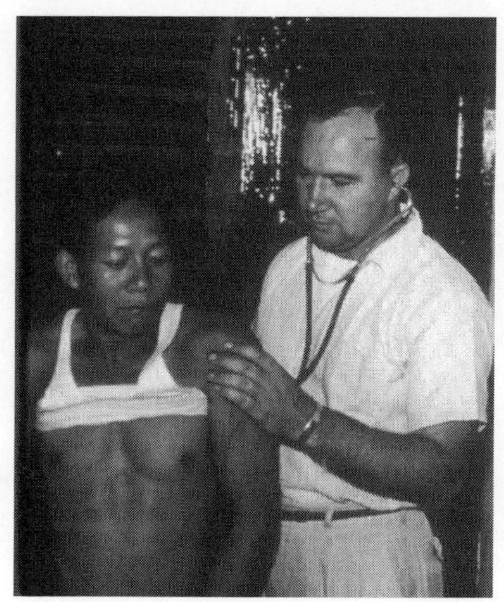

Figure 11

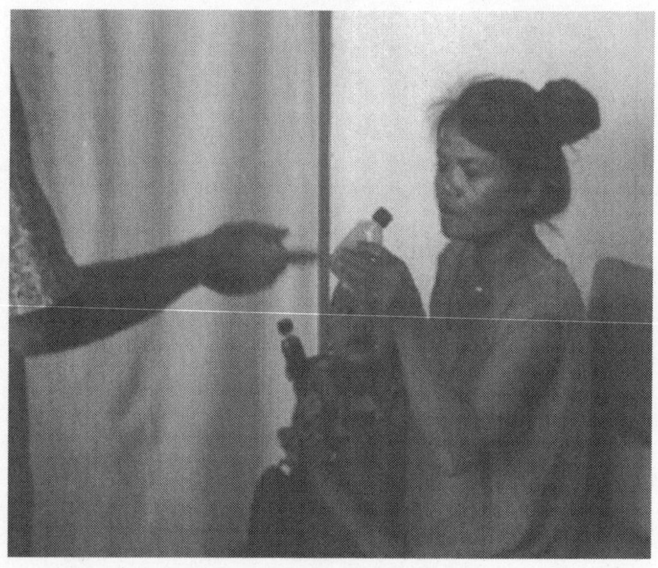

Figure 12

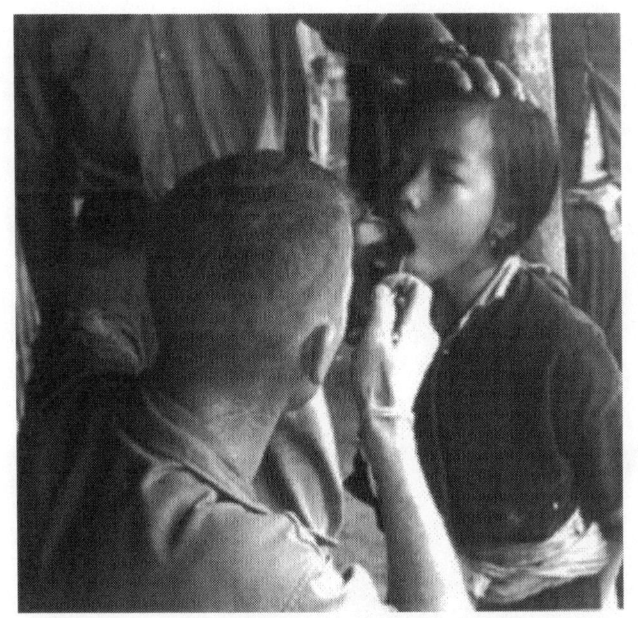

Figure 13

Figure 14

Figure 15

Figure 16

Figure 17

Figure 18

Figure 19

Figure 20

Figure 21

Figure 22

PART II

INTO LAOS—HOTFOOT & WHITESTAR

CHAPTER 11

LAOS: DIVINE KINGDOM

> *"...they were a dreamy, gentle, bucolic, non-aggressive people...who lived in bamboo and thatch houses on stilts, wading tranquilly in their marshy paddies, fishing in lazy rivers, and worshipping in the curly roofed pagodas. They are content. They live in a subsistence economy, and generally there is enough rice to go around. The Lao gentleness traditionally has enchanted the foreign visitor, particularly the one not trying to go anywhere or do anything in a hurry."*[128]
>
> *Oden Meeker*

Mountains and rivers dominate the Laotian landscape. The Annamite Mountain (*Phu Luang*) Chain rises 4,900 to 9,800 above sea level elevations. The rugged mountains form part of the country's eastern border with Vietnam, extending southward for two thirds of the country, eventually opening onto the 6,200 square mile Bolovens Plateau at the southern extremity of the country. The land is crisscrossed with multiple streams and rivers, cascading over falls deep in the heavily forested mountain terrain, eventually finding their way to the Mekong River (*Nam Khong*), which flows along the length of the county's western border. The lush jungle vegetation of triple canopied forest blocks all but a hint of the bright sun. The jungle opens up into clearings, from time to time, at various elevation peaks, resembling what is commonly found in the Eastern United States; thickets interspersed with deciduous and evergreen trees and shrubs.

The Laotian population consists of more than forty different ethnic cultures that are further divided by over a hundred sub-cultures. For simplicity's sake, the inhabitants of Laos can be loosely grouped into three geographic areas. The Lao Loum, Lowland Laotians, populate the plains and river valleys of the Mekong River and are the dominant political and cultural group. These regions are some of the most rugged terrain in the country, reaching elevations of about 4,500 feet. The Lao Theung inhabit the southern portion of the country near the Bolevens Plateau are in the extreme north along the borders of China and Vietnam. The Lao Sung occupy the high mountain peaks, living in small villages at elevations ranging from 4,000–9,000 feet. Buddhism is the predominant religion of the Lowland Lao. The Lao Theung and Lao Sung are animistic. One commonality among the three groups' is, village life revolves around the cycle of the monsoons and rice cultivation. The clearing, planting, weeding and harvesting of the crops demands daily attention.

The weather in Laos is attributed to the two distinct monsoon seasons; May through October is dry, November to April brings a range of temperatures that vary within the country according to altitude. The Mekong River Valley area experiences up to 100-degree heat from March to April and plunges to a low of 59 degrees during December and January. During the rainy season, temperatures average 84 degrees in the lowlands and 77 degrees in the mountain valleys. The extreme northeastern mountains can dip to a low of 30 degrees during the night in the dry season from November to February. The southern jungle areas remain relatively hot even during the 'cool' December dry spells and April is the hottest month throughout the country on average, with temperatures ranging between 72 degrees and a high of 95 degrees. The temperate monsoon climate creates an oasis filled with teak, Asian Rosewood and bamboo, teeming with exotic wildlife such as Asian Elephants, tigers, rhinoceros', monkeys and a multitude of other mammals. It is also home to thousands of species of birds, insects and some of the deadliest reptiles in the world, such as the krait and cobra. Special Forces medics were entering an enchanting but very dangerous environment. Their knowledge, skill and abilities would serve them well if they adapted to the environment and were willing to learn from the indigenous people inhabiting this strange land.

During SFC Patsy Angelone's tour, March 1962 to September 1962, he learned some fascinating medical information about some of these strange and exotic creatures.

> "This man came in to me and he looked like he had polio. One leg was thin and all wrinkled and the other was big and muscular. I did not even take a medical history on him. I figured the guy got polio. I took him down to Doc Meni[129] to tell him I can't use him (as a soldier), go ahead and discharge him. Doc Meni, he took one look at the leg and asks the guy, 'how long since the snake bit you?' That floored me! A snake? The guy said he got bit by a cobra. Doc told me when a cobra bites you it kills you within three hours. He said the muscle deteriorates. I asked what was the treatment for it and he replied, 'amputation.' Amputation is the only treatment for it. I never heard of that before. I never knew a snake could do that to you. I never treated many snakebites. Most of the snakebites were boas. I had one krait bite, but when he came in to me he was dead. A krait is like greased lightning. What makes it bad is like in the daytime you can step over a krait, he won't bother you. He is strictly a nocturnal snake. If it is a real cloudy day or cool day or in the evening, you won't even see him strike. It is just a blur and he has got you. Their bite is neuro-toxic. (Poisonous and destructive to nerve tissues)"[130]

The geography and climate of the country presented considerable challenges for the medics' proficiency as a "substitute" doctor operating in remote regions. When teams first arrived in Laos in 1959, the availability of air support for re-supply and evacuation was close to non-existent. Radio communications were limited due to the mountainous terrain and the few roads that existed, quickly became muddy impassable quagmires during the monsoon seasons. The monsoons dictated flying conditions for the few aircraft that were available for support of the remote teams. The teams relied heavily on the skill and bravery of the Air America supplied H-34 helicopters flown by Marine pilots, with a 'civilian' status, and the Civil Air Transport C-47's and DC 3's.

SGT Ned Miller, who served two tours in Laos, described the reliance of the teams located in remote locations upon those pilots.

> "Visualize Nam Tha as a little Dien Bien Phu, you would not be far from being correct, socked in for about six months out of the year on a flat valley surrounded on all sides by mountains. Our Air America helicopter pilots told us this; 'No matter how the weather is, no matter if you're socked in, we can get to you by following the rivers. We can get to you anytime.' We noticed these guys' shoes; every one of the Air America pilots had Marine and Navy type boon-dockers on. I used to be a Marine and I knew that was their shoe! Turned out 'yes' that was a squadron of Marines 'in the black' operating with Air America…After they came in and saved our fanny—we went in and bought 'em drinks all night!"[131]

The admiration and gratitude for the brave pilots is evident as Miller continued. "You get a team out there 75 clicks (Kilometers) from the nearest friendly, and they get over-run or they get hit hard and the friendly troops run, that leaves four or five Americans to fight their way out on their own. That's when good chopper people are worth their weight in gold."[132] The limited outside support added to the importance of the medics' ability to perform as a 'substitute doctor'. If something serious should happen to a team member, the team medic must be prepared to provide treatment until the patient could be evacuated. Attention from a physician was only accomplished through an emergency evacuation to either Clark Air Force Base in the Philippines, or the Seventh Day Adventist Hospital in Bangkok, Thailand.

CHAPTER 12

ANATOMY OF AN INSURGENCY

Why was Special Forces deployed to Laos? Understanding the political events assists in explaining why they were the perfect choice to carry out national policy. America became involved in Laos during the Eisenhower Administration. United States policy makers began providing foreign aid to countries under threat of communist insurgency, in an effort to counter irregular military forces being supported by the Soviet Union and China. These policies were the catalyst that enabled Special Forces to continue its existence as a unit and also catapulted them into the front lines of this new national policy. These jumbled, confusing political situations and covert aid programs created an environment in which Special Forces was trained to operate. Their activities were conducted, virtually without notice. Insurgency warfare began to take shape in Laos as the 1950's came to a close. Special Forces were chosen to help support the nation's political endeavors to halt the spread of communism. This required quiet diplomacy and the training of indigenous military forces.

The French defeat at Dien Bien Phu at the hands of the communist backed Viet Minh began a new struggle to contain communist expansion when the Geneva Accords of 1954 effectively ended French colonialism in Indochina. The Accords called for the division of Vietnam at the 17th parallel, creating North and South Vietnam. This placed Laos in the unique position of having a contiguous border with both the communist controlled North and the free, but near anarchist South. This proximity placed Laos center stage for the world's superpowers to claim as a prize. U.S. policy makers viewed Laos either as a buffer zone to ward off further communist expansion or as a sanctuary for insurgent forces to use as a base of operations for infiltration throughout Southeast Asia.

U.S. aid was first introduced and monitored in 1954 by the United States Information Service (USIS) and soon thereafter by the U.S. Operations Mission (USOM). Since a significant number of the problems faced by USOM at this time were military, a Programs Evaluation Office (PEO) was created in 1955. This semi-covert element was tasked with advising the Ambassador of Laos and the Chief of USOM on military matters, as well as overseeing the use of military material. The PEO operated covertly, directed by the CIA and the State Department, providing civilian cover as the means of entry for military personnel into Laos.

> "Initially the Programs Evaluation Office was very small, consisting of no more than a dozen retired and reserve military personnel in civilian status. This changed as the political instability of the Laotian government, its weak economy and the questionable effectiveness of the military training the Lao Army received through the French advisory effort. This political and military climate increased military assistance from the United States, including the covert use of active duty military personnel."[133]

Miller relates the team he deployed with wore "civilian clothes and carried State Department supplied civilian identification, the whole bit. On the second trip in, we were in uniform."[134]

In 1953 the Pathet Lao (Lao Peoples Liberation Army), supported by the Viet Minh, gained control of the two different provinces of Phong Saly and Sam Neua, which bordered the future North Vietnam. A year later, predicated by the Geneva Accords, the introduction of foreign military forces into Laos was restricted and provided for the integration of two Pathet Lao battalions, a total of 1,500 troops, into the Royal Lao

Army. The rest were to disband and be sent home. The French colonial forces were permitted to train and assist the newly formed Lao Army, Forces Armee du Royaume (FAR). The United States indirectly supported the French with funding and equipment through the provisions of the Mutual Defense Agreement.[135]

In 1957, the peace in Laos was precarious at best. The Government of National Union was created and the Pathet Lao was accorded representation in the government. The agreed upon Pathet Lao forces were preparing for integration into the FAR. In return, the Pathet Lao was to withdraw and return control of the two northern provinces to the Royal Lao Government. The special elections held in May 1958 resulted in significant support for the Pathet Lao. Because of this, the rightist elements of the new government were forced to compromise previous agreements. Soon, U.S. funding assistance was suspended, due to the unfavorable political climate.

In 1958, The Laotian budget was completely dependent upon U.S. funding.[136] The new government, Committee for the Defense of National Interests (CDNI), led by the rightist elements, excluded the Pathet Lao from both government representation and military integration into FAR. Just prior to the impending Pathet Lao May 1959 troop integration, one of the two battalions slipped away to the Plain of Jars during the night and was soon followed by the other battalion near Luang Prabang. The two battalions of Pathet Lao forces had fled to North Vietnam for regrouping, to conduct insurgent activities over the coming years.

In June 1959, the 'Heintges Plan'[137] created technological and logistical training programs conducted in Thailand by Filipino technicians, to upgrade the capabilities of the Laotian Army. FAR officers were also sent, for military training, to foreign countries including the United States. "The joint U.S.-French basic training program was to consist of divided responsibilities. The U.S. would be responsible for technical, including medical training and the French Military Mission would provide all tactical training."[138] Active duty military personnel, for the United States advisory role, operated under civilian cover because political prudence dictated that the introduction of large contingents of military personnel could possibly cause internal, as well as external repercussions. The first contingent of civilian clothed Special Forces teams arrived in the capital in Vientiane in July 1959. A 'C' Detachment remained in the capital city to provide support for the twelve, eight (8) man 'A' Detachments. The 'A' Detachments dispersed to the remote Royal Lao Army training centers located throughout the five Military Regions (MR). The program, code named 'HOTFOOT', officially designated the Lao Training Advisory Group (LTAG), introduced Special Forces soldiers as military advisors. Their mission was to provide training for the Lao Army in tactics of guerrilla warfare in an effort to counter the Pathet Lao should they attempt to overrun the country.

CHAPTER 13

OPERATIONS HOTFOOT and WHITESTAR

'HOTFOOT' operations in Laos began in July 1959 and continued through April 1961. New teams relieved the previous teams after their six-month TDY ended. This procedure continued after Aril 1961, when operations came out of 'the black' and the Special Forces teams exchanged civilian clothing for military uniforms. The 'HOTFOOT' teams underwent approximately two to three months of pre-mission training. The standard twelve-man detachments trained together, however, once training was completed, one half of the team deployed to Laos; the other half stayed behind as the relief unit, relieving the first team six months later. Ned Miller recalled, "We went as a reinforced team because we had mechanics with us. The other half stayed back to come on the next tour, next rotation, they came right on in."[139]

The uneasy peace that had existed during the first year of HOTFOOT operations was broken in August 1960 when the crack 2nd Parachute Battalion, led by Captain Kong Le, seized the administrative capital of Vientiane, aiming to establish a neutralist government. SGM Julius 'Dutch' Wyngaert recalled the professionalism of the unit, led by the charismatic leader;

> "He had the best damn battalion in all of Laos…The men were crazy about this guy. When they marched in there I thought they were German troops the way they stood. That guy hollered 'ATTENTION' and it was like a piece of marble standing

> there. They never moved they never batted an eyeball; when he said 'LEFT-FACE' it was like one—I could not believe it. These guys were really professionals...One morning I woke up and this guy took over the country; they had troops coming in from the south, but they came as far as the city limits and that was it. He had troops stationed all over the electric plant, the radio stations, at the government offices. He was there and he wanted the Americans to back him. He was going to nail the black marketeering, etc."[140]

General Phoumi Nosavan and Prince Boun Oum led a coalition of anticommunist and neutralist forces in opposition to King Le to retake the capital. The PEO backed the coalition after discovering Kong Le had requested aid from Soviet bloc countries and made overtures of alliance toward the communist backed Pathet Lao after the U.S. had refused to back his coup attempt. Several Field Training Teams accompanied the anti-Kong Le forces, marking the first time U.S. combat forces participated in active combat operations in Laos. The four day battle that ensued to recapture Vientiane began on December 13, 1960. Kong Le's forces fought a delaying action to safely evacuate toward Luang Prabang in the north. By December 16, 1960, with his men and equipment intact, Pathet Lao and North Vietnamese forces joined them.

Aided by Soviet airlifts of supplies, Kong Le combined forces with the Pathet Lao and launched a successful campaign against the forces of Phoumi Nosavan on January 1, 1961, taking control of the Plain of Jars and nearly overran Laos by the Spring of 1961. Negotiations in Geneva during May 1961 only took place after the United States issued a warning to the Soviets of possible intervention to forestall the possible communist takeover of Laos. By April 1961 a Military Assistance and Advisory Group (MAAG) was formed and the covert nature of Special Forces participation was brought out into the open. HOTFOOT operations were re-designated as WHITE STAR Mobile Training Teams (WSMTT) in September 1962, and the 'civilians' that had been training FAR troops put on their uniforms.

The eight man detachments from HOTFOOT deployments reverted back to their traditional strength of twelve men, enabling them to operate as split teams, thus doubling their efforts and capabilities. Special Forces medics now began to conduct medical civic action activities among the Lao people in villages and hamlets, their movement no longer restricted to the military training centers. 'B' Detachments deployed to each of the Military Regions providing additional support and as a liaison between the 'A' Detachments and the 'C' Detachment based in Vientiane, coordinating support and supplies. The 'B' Detachment composition was still being organized as a part of the Special Forces operational structure and struggled to define it's role during deployments. SFC Clarence W. McCormick was assigned to the split B Detachments stationed in Thakhet. McCormick remembered his role was generally spent supporting the 'A' Detachments in the field. But, the majority of his time was spent riding helicopters delivering non-medical supplies, such as gasoline and food. Another lesson was being learned in Laos for the support units that would eventually provide valuable assistance in Vietnam to the 'A' Detachment medics.

The U.S. role increased dramatically after the Geneva Agreements forced the departure of French forces and aid, leaving a large void. The U.S. quickly filled this void with both material and men. This change allowed for the men to 'get back to basics' with guerrilla forces waging warfare against the Pathet Lao and Viet Minh. Special Forces teams were no longer restricted to the Regional Military Training Centers and began to get out into the countryside with the FAR troops in a new role as tactical and technical advisors for operations.

WHITESTAR teams most often operated as split detachments. This left one medic per team operating in a dual medical and combatant role. As the war in Laos continued the teams experienced higher levels of enemy activity. The heightened exposure to hostile fire and the differences between 'HOTFOOT' and 'WHITESTAR' operations was punctuated in early March 1961. Captain Walter Moon's FTT-59 (Field Training Team), attached to the 6th Royal Laotian Army Battalion d'Infanterie, at Ban Pha Home were engaged in a running battle against

Kong Le's troops on the Plain of Jars. On April 22, 1961, at Pho Teaso, the battalion came under heavy artillery fire and was subsequently surrounded and overrun by the Pathet Lao. Captain Moon was captured during the initial attack. Surrounded, SFC John Bischoff (Medic) and SGT Gerald Biber (Radio Operator) attempted a breakout by climbing aboard an armored car headed south on Route 13. "According to Lao survivors, they crouched behind the turret, but the car came under heavy grenade attack. SFC Bischoff fired a machine gun from the vehicle until he was shot through the neck and killed. SGT Biber had already been wounded and was apparently killed by stick grenades thrown against the armored car."[141] SGT Orville Ballinger (Demolitions) escaped into the jungle with other Lao soldiers. Seven days later the Pathet Lao captured them several miles down river on a boat they had found. SGT Ballinger, held with Captain Moon, was eventually released in August 1962. He reported that Captain Moon attempted to escape twice from captivity. During his final escape attempt he suffered chest and head wounds. After several long months of mistreatment and abuse, Captain Moon was executed in his jail cell in Lat Theoung on July 22, 1962. The bodies of Sergeant's Bischoff and Biber were never found and remain missing to this day.

At the same time Captain Moon and SGT Ballinger were still being held prisoner, Field Training Teams throughout Laos encountered increased Pathet Lao activity. Medical SSG Don Dougan recalls a Sunday morning around 4 o'clock the Pathet Lao commenced a mortar attack on the Officer Candidate Training School in Dong Hene. Sunday was normally a leisurely day for both the Americans and the Pathet Lao so; the attack came as quite a surprise, since no enemy patrols or activity had been spotted in the area for some time. Dougan recalls;

> "The attack came from the south-east…This happened prior to the 2nd Geneva Accords in Paris in May of 1962, I believe. There were only minor casualties on our side and we never learned how many KIA/WIA (Killed in Action/Wounded in Action) the PL (Pathet Lao) took. They were about 200–300 meters

away, estimated company size, in an open area. We had built mortar pits reinforced with logs and dirt around the south side of the camp where 60mm mortars were emplaced. We also had two, 81mm heavy mortars in position. It should be noted that at this point in time, the Lao had no real desire to make physical contact with the PL and although we had pinpointed where they had gone, the Lao Commanders circumvented our efforts to catch up with them or counter-attack. It was a most peculiar time; nothing was clear-cut either politically or militarily. It was only another four of five months before all WHITESTAR teams were pulled out of Laos."[142]

CHAPTER 14

TAILORED FOR SPECIAL FORCES

A basic concept of guerrilla or insurgent warfare is for a guerrilla force to incite, encourage or coerce the local population to support the insurgency. The philosophy of an insurgent movement is to discredit the current government among the local population. The insurgent forces must gain the support of the population. An insurgency attempts to convince the populace that the new government will bring the people the things they want, need and deserve after the current government is overthrown and replaced by the 'people's movement'. This is generally accomplished by exploiting the current government's internal weakness. Most often, corruption within the high echelons of power is the root cause in fomenting dissatisfaction among the population.

To militarily counter the insurgent tactics the troubled nation accepts foreign aid and assistance. Special Forces provides a highly effective, cost effective low visibility means to extend military aid through a concept known as force multipliers. This means a small number of experts arm and train an indigenous people to protect themselves and support the current government against insurgent activities. They also show the people how to improve their everyday living conditions by establishing civic action programs. Establishing medical assistance programs rank high on the priority list for Special Forces teams entering a host nation. Medical treatment usually wins the trust of the people and provides almost instantaneous results. The men of Special Forces are there to provide the 'know how' within the villages, so that the people can continue strengthening their communities and ultimately supporting the government once Special Forces leaves. The medics' role addresses, among many others, preventable conditions, such as, mal-nourishment and the resulting vitamin deficiencies which increases susceptibility to many illnesses and diseases. In most cases there is a simple remedy that the medic can institute to address the cause of the problem. Among the most effective methods reducing these afflictions is to develop a means of providing locally available dietary staple and improving sanitation conditions. This also reduces a future dependency situation for the villagers that would require long term outside support to maintain.

President John F. Kennedy chose Special Forces for this type of warfare because he felt that the proud and elite unit could carry out his vision and ideas of improved U.S. capabilities for conducting paramilitary operations and unconventional warfare. In President Kennedy, Special Forces found a supporter who understood and appreciated not only the symbolism of the "Beret", but the abilities of those who wore it to address the growing concern with communist backed insurgencies. The use of Special Forces was a logical response to the new counter insurgency concept being employed where insurgencies were taking place, with Vietnam leading the list. The Commander in Chief supported the Special Forces mission and catapulted them from their relatively unknown existence, to spearhead the new United States political strategy. The American press, along with books and movies, cast them to the front of the public consciousness. Their preferred low profile and secretive nature would now be difficult to maintain.

The introduction of Special Forces teams to Laos as military advisors heralded a new age of warfare for the U.S. The new and relatively alien concept of advisor/counter insurgency warfare was generally an untested change from the original doctrine of teams operating behind enemy lines in a conventional warfare scenario. Special Forces realized the ideal opportunity to organize and train an indigenous guerrilla force capable and willing to fight for their homes and families that existed among the ethnic minority tribesmen occupying the tactically important

Bolovens Plateau and the Plain of Jars region. The Hmong and Kha tribes had been continuously harassed and agitated by Pathet Lao and Viet Minh cadre seeking to exploit that same guerrilla potential. The Hmong had been resisting the communist incursions since before 1954. They were a part of the broad cultural group of the Lao Sung, and are one of six ethnic tribes, numbering approximately 200,000, accounting for two-thirds of the country population.

Their settlements were mostly located in the northern part of the country with some small clans extending as far south as Vientiane. Their villages were typically comprised of approximately 20–30 households built directly on the ground on land that is selected according to the principles of geomancy. Hmong society is sub-divided into several sub-cultures that are usually named for the color of their traditional dress, White, Red, Green and Striped. Pigs, chickens and cattle graze in the surrounding fields of the village with little to no supervision. The people's common belief that a spirits contentment or discontentment, control the welfare of everything in the village, including illness'. Shamans are respected and held in high regard within the village. The shamans provide spiritual guidance and serve as healers who can treat spirit induced illness. They have been 'chosen' by the spirits after having suffered a long illness themselves. These very simple and private people had originally fled China to escape persecution and political campaigns. They were now once again, caught up in political turmoil that they truly had no desire to be a part of. Their individualism and years of persecution by the lowland Lao made them ideal candidates for recruitment by either the Pathet Lao or the United States in the support of a new government in Laos. The Pathet Lao had harassed and mistreated them for many years in their attempt to take control of northern Laos. The introduction of Special Forces, who brought medicine, food and arms to help them defend against the Pathet Lao taking their land and food created a manpower pool that had a potential for organization into a paramilitary force.

Further to the south is the Kha tribe. The Kha had different reasons to accept training offered to them. There had been a longstanding animosity between the Kha and the ruling Lao. The Lao considered them savages and the Kha had been treated as such for many years. Seizing on this opportunity, the initial discussions between Special Forces and Kha tribal leaders led to the first FTT's being introduced into the region during January 1962. The highly classified training program, known as 'Operation Pincushion' was completely controlled by Special Forces. Security and training integrity was of vital importance to this program. This program required selected tribesmen to be taken to remote training centers located at the eastern edge of the Bolovens Plateau for five weeks of Special Forces developed tactical training. FTT's recruited, organized and trained units of a hundred men each. Once trained, they were returned to their villages to conduct missions, which included harassment, elimination of enemy units, interdiction of the Ho Chi Minh Trail and securing of intelligence concerning enemy movements.

Al Maggio recalls his team first worked out of Lao Nam in Military Region IV, east of Pakse, training a Lao Army 'Battalion d' Infantrie. The team then moved to the Bolovens Plataeu to train five companies of Kha tribesmen in guerrilla warfare tactics as part of 'Operation Pincushion'. Each trainee received some limited medical training that centered mainly on sanitation and hygiene practices. An additional thirty-five hours of training was provided for selected personnel to increase their potential as unit medics. Once training was completed, a company sized unit was led by two Special Forces members back to their villages to patrol along the trails leading into South Vietnam. Al Maggio relates an event while out on patrols with the Kha that is a good example of the medics' observations that added to the knowledge about the country for the benefit of future teams.

> "The area the Kha were from, villagers grew a plant that tasted like tapioca pudding. It was called 'Bread Fruit', it grows as big as a small pumpkin, but it's green. There were round pockets of eatable parts. The tribesmen always ate it when we passed through a village orchard. You break it open with your hands and chew the sweet parts, *tastes like tapioca and real good*."[143]

The training that Special Forces teams were now conducting with the indigenous tribes presented situations that required the medic to fulfill a dual role of soldier and healer. As an example, while on patrol with a company of Kha Tribesmen, Maggio earned the Combat Infantry Badge (CIB). An excerpt from the commendation describes how the medics often found themselves performing as an infantry leader.

> "Due to operational commitments of the detachment in the Kha Program during the period 1 April–25 September 1962, it was necessary to assign SFC Maggio as Senior Infantry Advisor to Company K8, Kha Tribesmen. During this period SFC Maggio accompanied K8 on all operations and was under enemy small arms fire on numerous occasions and specifically on 30 August 1962, in the vicinity of Bon Tayune, Laos, while accompanying a combat patrol that was ambushed by Communist Pathet Lao forces."[144]

It must be reiterated, and understood that all medics are not only capable, but also expected, to perform in this dual capacity. Many of the medics found themselves in similar situations, but were never awarded medals or recognized for their acts of bravery. This was a part of being Special Forces. Most of the men were operating in highly sensitive areas. Bringing attention to their deeds would have exposed much of what they were doing and where they were operating and could have jeopardized their missions.

Angelone described the expanded role the medics encountered in Laos. "I had two jobs. I ran sick call in the morning and I spent the afternoon training rifle companies in small unit tactics. These two jobs combined and made a third. One program was initiated in conjunction with the Lao Colonel in charge of the FAR battalion they were advising."[145] The team was operating in the Nam Son River Valley, which empties into the Mekong River along the Thailand border. The valley areas of Laos are rich in rice production and the Nam San was no different. At harvest time, the Pathet Lao came into the villages and stole the rice from the villagers. Angelone would travel with another Special

Forces soldier up the Nam San River, treating villagers along the way, conducting sick calls in the villages they passed through. "I would spend two or three days there and win over the people with medicine."[146] The rest of the team would follow behind them, and distribute rifles and machine guns. They would teach the villagers how to use them so that they could protect their rice crops and prevent them from being conscripted into the Pathet Lao Army. "It was pretty successful because by the time we got through going up that Nam San, these villagers were armed and trained for village defense."[147] The ultimate goal was to to force the Pathet Lao to come en-mass to take things from the villagers, instead of just sending a cadre of a few men. The villagers could defend themselves long enough for a larger FAR force to arrive. Conducting repeated sick calls in the villages 'won' the people's trust. In most cases, this was the first occasion any of the villagers had seen western medicine at work. Usually, the older women of the village would seek treatment first. Then, the other women would come and bring their children, after seeing the older women beginning to get better. Finally, the men and the boys would stop being leery and come to sick call. "To me, that was the whole success in the program. Once we gave the stuff that started curing them and they started getting better. They started trusting us"[148], remembers Angelone.

There was also a humanitarian effort within 'Operation Pincushion'. Civic action programs were introduced into the local villages to augment the Kha training program. They were designed to enhance the impact of the U.S. presence and foster a positive relationship with the Kha. This was done through repeated visits by medics, emphasizing the availability of medical care for all the Kha units and their families. The Hmong, in the north, underwent similar training at training centers, but did not operate under such covert conditions. Medical training for the Hmong was covered a little more extensively. It included hygiene, sanitation, water purification, bandaging, splinting, treatment for shock and evacuation methods. All of these programs served as models that would become a very important integral part of Special Forces operations in Vietnam.

The importance and impact of both the HOTFOOT and WHITESTAR operations upon Special Forces operations can not be overstated. They gained invaluable experience from their first foray into counter insurgency. In particular, the medical experience and knowledge gained would play a huge role during the war that was developing in Vietnam. Dr. David Paulsrud, one of the surgeons accompanying teams to Laos, candidly summarized the medics dedication, effort and performance. "Our medics were often the most respected member of the team, as far as the indigenous people were concerned. This was heady stuff for the medics, like it is for a doctor when he first starts seeing patients."[149] Medical information gathered and reviewed from post-mission debriefings resulted in a tremendous impact upon medical training procedures and deployment considerations. Many new demands were encountered teaching medicine and sanitation practices under duress of cultural resistance and hostile fire conditions. The HOTFOOT and WHITESTAR teams recognized language and cultural differences as topics that must be targeted during pre-deployment training procedures. Additionally, the medics' role within the team, gaining the confidence and support of the people, became an integral part to understanding the people, their culture and their medical problems.

CHAPTER 15

GROWING AN ARMY

The HOTFOOT teams encountered many operational difficulties. First, there was a convoluted chain of command, tangled with bureaucratic red tape that infringed upon Special Forces instructional training time. Second, the lines of communication and coordination between the multiple agencies and organizations, such as the Laotian Army, the French Military Mission, U.S. Ambassador and the commander for each of the FAR Military regions were chaotic at best. The restrictions placed upon their activities by the various competing authorities ran counter to the Special Forces propensity to work within its own organizational support system. Superior Special Forces communication capabilities often enabled them to bypass the multiple regional authorities throughout the country. Also hampering their efforts was limited time. The limited training time of 115 total hours to train medics placed considerable limitations on subjects of instruction.

The 'HOTFOOT' medical mission was seemingly simple and relatively uncomplicated. It was to provide medical care for the LTAG Teams and conduct basic medical familiarization training for Laotian Army personnel. Groups of Lao Army soldiers received training during a seven-week cycle. Of that seven weeks, ten hours of instructional time was allotted for the medics to provide training in field sanitation, personal hygiene and first aid subjects. The medical portion of the overall training was scheduled to take place during the first two weeks of the seven week cycle, in hopes that the training could be put to use by the Lao soldiers during the remainder of the training cycle. An additional six hours of medical training was conducted for select Laotian Army personnel targeted to be designated as unit medics. The system left little time to assess the impact of the training among the trainees.

The medic also had to rely on an interpreter to present his course to a student body comprised mostly of illiterate people from multiple ethnic and religious cultures, further restricting the flow of information. The use of interpreters, vital to the mission, also reduced the probable effectiveness of the medics' efforts, because their actual instruction time was further reduced by the convoluted attempts at translation. Classes were taught, to the multi-ethnic composition of the Laotian Army units, in Laotian or French and through the use of Thai interpreters, who possessed a limited knowledge of English medical terms, further compounding frustrations. Added to this complex language barrier was the fact that the Special Forces medics only had a limited command of either French or Laotian. Ned Miller explains that there was language training during pre-mission training, as well as training in the use of interpreters. He also added that this seemingly large obstacle was overcome by a simplistic approach. "If you could learn to speak ten usable sentences, you're on your way to learning a good chunk of your every day by day part of a language. You can go 'past, present, future' and keep building on it."[150]

Another medical NCO, SGT Fred Hardy serving in Laos (April 1961 to October 1961) recalled, "I would talk to a…person who maybe fought with the French and another guy had been down the mountain and he knows a little Laotian and maybe they understand each others dialect… but can you imagine this guy understanding a little Laotian, but the guy he is talking to doesn't understand Laotian…so he goes from maybe the other guy who spoke a little French (*to someone else*)…so what we had was about a four person round robin and being translated four different times. None of us knew what we were talking about, so I was probably treating the guy for hangnail with a headache pill. I had no idea…"[151] Perhaps Earle Peckham, best summarizes the importance of language skills to complete the team mission in the advisory capacity. "You were nothing but a school teacher. You had to be able to impart your information through an interpreter or direct language to an individual in an operational area. If you couldn't do that, you were useless."[152] This lesson would not be lost in translation in training recommendations.

Adding to an already difficult situation there was also, at times, a lack of motivation and an inability or unwillingness of Lao officers to convince the trainees that there was urgency to the training. The Laotian people are by nature, generally non-violent and unable to comprehend the need for violence to defend their selves against the highly motivated Pathet Lao. The Pathet Lao, on the other hand, employed harsh tactics of coercion against the villagers to garner their support. When faced with the brutality employed by the communists, the gentle Lao generally capitulated. Ned Miller described the harsh reality of what was taking place in the jungles of Laos with blunt accuracy;

> "The Vietnamese and Pathet Lao leaders could bring stronger persuasion to bear. They could take the first person [who refused to understand the urgency of cooperation] out behind the bunker and shoot him in the head. Then they could take the second person out behind the bunker and shoot him in the head. Pretty soon, number three realized he better do what he is told."[153]

Earle Peckham further described the horrors that occurred in the villages and what Special Forces role was to counter the terror campaign being waged by the insurgents. "The Pathet Lao were raping and stealing them [villagers] from their villages. It was Special Forces job to convince the villagers that we weren't interested in that type of activity."[154]

Ned Miller explained the role of advisor and how the men had to be ambassadors who represented ideas and different ways to accomplish goals and how the role of advisor fit quite naturally to the Special Forces mission. "our mission in life was to train guerrillas and partisans, where we worked with the Laotians, the Cubans and all the other different countries. It just came as second nature. Teacher, recommender; they have questions and you've got an answer. It is second nature to very tactfully recommend 'so and so' or 'what do you think about this?' and you lay out a plan and 'oh, that is a fantastic idea you got there sir'. You never tried to make them lose face."[155]

Losing face was an important part of cultural society among the Lao, if not handled appropriately the results could be devastating. For example, the lack of awareness to Lao cultural differences when encountering a seemingly mundane task of deciding where to dig holes for a latrine could produce a potentially damaging environment. 'Dutch' Wyngaert recalled that he once suggested the battalion chief medic should close the old latrines and dig new ones. Wyngaert explained to the Lao medic that his should be done since the unit had not moved from its encampment for a considerable amount of time and would soon present general health problems. After the Lao medic did this, a confrontation between the U.S. advisors and the Lao battalion commander erupted. The battalion commander felt he had 'lost face' because his command prerogative had been infringed upon by the American advisor suggesting and directing one of his soldiers. The Lao commander had "not been directly consulted on if, when, where or how the latrines needed to be relocated."[156] Wyngaert explained that the Americans were there to advise, not take over or take charge. "The approval of the battalion commander; you must always have approval of the highest command before you do anything. If you don't, this guy will really give you problems like you never had before."[157] A simple assumption could compromise a team's mission due to cultural differences. In this case, "Those Americans don't run these battalions!"[158], was the perceived threat by the Lao battalion commander. Recognizing this type of situation required mature, fast thinking to defuse and provide a means to 'save face'. Wyngaert explained to the irate commander, "I suggested it to him that we ought to do it, and he ought to see *someone.* I did not say to him 'he ought to see somebody.' I thought he was going to do it, see somebody; but he didn't, he just went ahead and did it."[159] Wyngaert learned from the innocent oversight to never make an assumption when talking to the Lao troops. The battalion commander had the Laotian soldier dig all of the latrines alone. The reprimanded Lao medic held no ill feelings for Wyngaert. 'Dutch' explained to the Lao medic that when he himself had an idea, he had to get approval from his team leader before doing something also. That just because he said something didn't mean for him to go ahead and do it without asking his boss first.

Cultural beliefs and practices often-resulted in reluctance by FAR troops to engage in combat. This was not rooted in cowardice, but a cultural tendency "to react to the superstitious and subscribe to mass hysteria even when suffering light casualties. One report provides an example of the Laotian 'phi', which is a belief in spiritual intervention, a significant part of Lao culture. This belief caused physically uninjured casualties who suffered the loss of 'friendly spirits' from the close passage of a bullet or a nearby explosion of mortar rounds."[160] The FAR troops considered these 'casualties' a priority for evacuation that must be taken quickly to a temple so "a Buddhist priest could restore the 'spirit' to its protecting position."[161] When poor leadership was combined with this religious induced hysteria, it could lead to near disaster.

One such instance occurred during the battle of Nam Tha in May 1962. Ned Miller described it as sheer panic. Shortly before the fall of Nam Tha, Detachment FTT-1 was operating with the 11th Group Mobile in the mountainous region south of the village. On the morning that the village fell to Pathet Lao forces Miller had taken a MAAG Colonel and Laotian General to the airstrip for evacuation. During his return trip through the town he passed the Lao Army and Police Headquarters buildings. The town was deserted. Everyone was headed along a rough jeep road to make the 75 kilometer trip into neighboring Burma.

Once he made it back to the team house, the Americans had to decide which route of escape was best. If they attempted to catch up with the retreating Lao Battalion that had just suffered a withering battle defeat against the Pathet Lao, they stood the chance of being mistaken for enemy elements, in pursuit of the routed Laotians, and being shot by the spooked soldiers. The best option seemed to be to head north toward the Hmong village Miller had first visited, and follow a foot trail into Burma.

As the Pathet Lao, led by North Vietnamese advisors, advanced against the village, the Americans scrambled to destroy as much equipment and supplies as possible. The ensuing escape is best relayed through Millers recollections.

> "As we headed out across the rice paddies, toward the north of Nam Tha, there was a police jeep stuck in a ditch—right where we had to cross—we rammed him out of the way, flat crashed into him and knocked him outta the way. Then we drove on up the mountain to that little Hmong village. It was totally deserted. I had just run sick call up there the day before. So, they knew the bad guys were coming too. We shot two holes in the gas tanks and burned the jeeps right there. The Air America helicopters were coming back in from Luang Prubang. We got one of the radios working. 'DO NOT, REPEAT, DO NOT LAND AT THE TEAMHOUSE. THE BAD GUYS HAVE IT. IF YOU LOOK OUT YOUR LEFT WINDOW TO THE HILLSIDE, YOU'LL SEE SMOKE. THAT'S US. YOU'LL SEE A LITTLE VILLAGE UP HERE.' It was old Marine Corps helicopters, either H-34 or 37's, they came on up. There was two of them and they circled down in through that triple canopy where that village was and flew us back to Luang Prabang."[162]

While Miller's team was attempting to exfiltrate, another half detachment (FTT 1-A), stationed down in Sayaboury began preparing to infiltrate by parachute with hopes of stopping the stampede of the Lao Army into Burma. But, prior to being able to get 'chuted up and dropped in', the masses began moving toward Burma once again. Miller recalls the tragic scene that unfolded, "When they got down to the river, the Mekong, about 400 of them got drowned by panicking and overloading the boats."[163] FTT-1 and FTT-1A rendezvoused back in Sayaboury for a few weeks of rest while a plan was being developed to attempt a counter attack.

Of the 6,000 troops that fled into Burma, approximately 400 were convinced to return to Laos to continue the fight. Of the 400, 75 were compelled to take part in the counter-offensive to retake the village.

After re-equipping in Ban Huoei Sai they headed back north to Nam Tha. Miller recalls,

> "I don't know the name of the little village that all this took place…We had the mission of taking 25, out of the 75.[164] There were four of us and one interpreter. About half of the 25 indigenous troops were 'auto defense' and the other half regular Lao Army. Our job was to go forward and make contact. We walked *ALL NIGHT LONG* and into the next morning. Quite early the next morning, just as it was beginning to turn daylight, We seen this little kid. We knew there was a little village up the road a little ways. Through the interpreter we asked the little kid if the Pathet Lao were in the village and he said, 'yes'. With the interpreter, and a couple others, they went up and talked to the kid's father up in the field where he was working. 'Is there any bad guys in the village?' the interpreter asks. Dad says 'Oh no, no, no.' Well, we felt innocence and truth, and fear, were two different things. We got our heads together and decided we better drop back a little bit to a better position and set up at least temporarily and then decide what we wanted to do.
>
> We fell back about a mile, crossed a little stream and set up. Of course the troops with us had to cook their rice to eat. They had their fire going and were cooking, and I said to Captain Johnson; 'Sir, we better get these people into position of some kind.' He said, 'OK, would you go ahead and do that?' I went ahead and got them all in position except those right at the fire. It wasn't two minutes later we got hit by about 200 of 'em. It turned out to be three companies of them, but we didn't know that right then.
>
> The 'auto defense' fought pretty good, valley people [Lao Army] just took off and ran immediately. The five or six of us were just leap-frogging back, just making sure…taking care of ourselves—that was all there was to it. There was a little tiny jeep road going through there and it was up around the first

> curve where I seen 'Tex' Simmons step across a guy named Vince O'Rourke, he stepped across him, Vince was down in a firing position. I saw three tracers go between 'Tex's' legs, and that should be about 15 bullets if I counted right, at least 10. [These two men still joke to this day about that incident: anytime Tex says he is 'Too Tall' Simmons, I says, 'no you're not buddy, you're just right'] Just a little bit after that Tex asks Captain Johnson, 'Would you like me to stop those people because that is on up toward the mountain top?' Tex is about 6 foot 6 inches tall, takes about six foot strides. Captain Johnson says, 'Well, give it a try.' Tex took off up that mountain. About an hour later when we finally got up to 'em, this mountain range we were going over, Tex had all 25 of 'em stopped at bayonet point! At least we came back into that village as a group anyway."[165]

FTT-1 returned to Ban Huoei Sai for some rest. FTT-2 went up to the small village where the skirmish had taken place between the Pathet Lao and FTT-1. On March 27, 1962, Miller recalls,

> "Three companies of Pathet Lao hit that little village and that is when the two Americans got lost (SGT Murphy and Loobey)[166] 'Course we couldn't let that happen. We got all three half detachments (FTT-1, FTT-2 and FTT-2A), about 14 people plus interpreters and about 75 Laotians, half 'auto defense, half regular (Lao Army) to start working in on the counter attack. We hit 'em hard enough to get their attention, because they fell back out of the village. I think what was really frosting on the cake was the three or four Air America helicopters started flying way off over to the west toward the village, the helicopters were in a row, and they'd set down as if they were bringing in more reinforcements—they were empty, but the bad guys didn't know that!
>
> We flew over the village and started running search patterns looking for those two guys [missing SF]. Well, a day or two

> later they were picked up down on the Mekong River, straight south of there, miles and miles away. They signaled a helicopter with a mirror…they had heard us counter-attack, but there were just too many bad guys between them and us and they just couldn't come back through that way. They just E and E'ed straight on south, they came out of it alright."[167]

The most frustrating experiences the teams encountered lied within the inherent lack of leadership among the lowland Lao troops. Through training, the hill tribes were quite adept acquiring the skills from training to fight a guerrilla war. The Lao tendency to lead quiet and peaceful lives negated the desire to fight such a war. Ned Miller explains some of the frustrations felt by the advisors,

> "Some of the valley Laotians would fight as long as they were led properly. But if they know their leaders are stealing them blind every payday and they're getting less rations, less food, less everything, they're going to tend to say, 'why me?' When properly led, they would do a lot better. Any unit that is led by a more capable officer or NCO would be better. There was one battalion south and back to the east of Pakse at a placed called Attipeu. The whole battalion was led by a Sergeant Major and a very effective unit. Leadership is a bunch of it."[168]

The common denominator for the Laotian Army unit's ineffectiveness was the lack of leadership. This was demonstrated well by the 'Auto Defense', Lowland Lao troops, who fought alongside the American advisors during the 'WHITE STAR' Operations. Ned Miller said, "There were some awfully good people. There were people who had been trained here in the States. Gone through the infantry school. Some had gone through the schools in France. There were some professional military people in there who had fought with the French against the Viet Minh. The politically strong were the ones who got promoted, those politically strong people were not always the best leaders."[169]

CHAPTER 16

CULTURAL AWARENESS

Special Forces experiences in Laos provided extensive lessons regarding the unique cultural aspects peculiar to Southeast Asia, "special care must be taken to not embarrass students in front of their counterparts for any negative or wrong answers, in order to avoid them 'losing face'."[170] A critical part of their job was teaching the students how to be teachers themselves, to enable them to conduct training of new students on their own. If a student teacher made a mistake in a presentation, the medic simply made a note of the error and informed the student during the next break. 'Dutch' Wyngaert explained that "you never interrupted right in the middle of class."[171] Understanding this cultural difference would be very important to the medics, because the growing involvement in Southeast Asia would present countless situations in which this knowledge and the ability to make conditions conducive to the furtherance of their medical mission played a vital role in their success, or failure.

During SFC Julius 'Dutch' Wyngaert's first tour (July 1959 to January 1960) his team trained members of the Royal Lao Army in the vicinity of Pakse. His mornings usually consisted of conducting sick call. The cases were mainly infections, dysentery and "they were all infested with parasites, hook worms, pin worms, etc."[172] Training usually started after 1 p.m. by getting all the medics from the battalion together for medical class. He found that by listening to the Lao medic, no matter how outlandish the complaint from a patient; such as worms in their ears or having the devil inside of them helped gain their friendship, trust and cooperation. By acting unaware of the illness being described and asking the Lao medic what should be done for the particular problem, Wyngaert, gave the appearance that the Lao medic was more knowledgeable about a subject. By doing this, Wyngaert wasn't projecting himself as the "big American" coming in and forcing himself on everyone. For him to have done so was a prescription for failure and being unwelcome. He summed up this prevailing philosophy; "It obtains the same results. Let them do it their way; what difference does it make because it makes them look good."[173]

'Saving face' would be a difficult hurdle to clear for the non-commissioned officer who was able to perform advanced techniques that high ranking military or civilian Laotian doctors had not ever encountered before. The number of foreign-trained physicians in Laos, as late as 1971, was fewer than fifteen.

> "The four year medical training program at Vientiane was initiated in 1957 to produce doctors with limited skills, not readily comparable with their western counterparts. By United States Army standards, the training of FAR medical personnel was inadequate. Their level of expertise varied at every level. For example, FAR battalion surgeons ranked high in prestige but low in technical expertise in comparison to their U.S. equivalents. Most were comparable in training to U.S. Army enlisted medics. From that level, the proficiency declined sharply as far as the unit medic was concerned. Some of the battalion surgeons acquired their training from the French and were very reluctant to accept any further guidance or advice. Many of the French techniques differed from those employed in the United States, and there was a generally preconceived belief among the Laotians that the French methods of treatment were superior. Often these Laotian beliefs ran counter to the well-proven methods. As a result, U.S. medicines and methods were frequently rejected. A prime example was the Lao belief that administration of dextrin [which is actually a plasma expander

used in lieu of blood available for transfusion into a patient suffering shock from loss of blood] causes shock."[174]

Laotian Army medical personnel had no systematic or standardized procedures for qualifying aidmen. Soldiers were often assigned to duties without the necessary training. "The problem was especially acute at the lower echelons, such as on the battalion or company level. The results were self explanatory."[175]

Another condition, adding to the complexity of the medics mission was that of the religious and superstitious beliefs of the villagers. These very powerful forces must be recognized, understood and implemented into the work of the medic. Some of the beliefs are universal throughout Laos; others are unique within the local area, as an example, the innocent act of placing your hand on a villager's head. It is not uncommon for an American soldier to do this when greeting children. In some instances, this was taboo in Laos. Angelone recalled that the best way to ascertain the various cultural oddities of a village was to have the interpreter find out from the FAR troops what these peculiarities may be. In some villages it was taboo to step on the porch of a hut, unless invited. Two miles away at the next village it could be an insult not to step up on the porch.[176]

Spiritual beliefs were almost surreal, for example, an interpreter once explained to Angelone the reasoning a man had for refusing evacuation until his foot, blown off by a land mine, was cremated. "You had to be cremated to come back to life…this guy, if we did not cremate his foot, he would not let us evacuate him…because he figured 'When I come back I ain't going to have a foot because you buried it.'"[177] The simplest of medical procedures could be hindered by these beliefs that were completely foreign to the medic. Indigenous personnel from the village of Nam Tha believed that their hair could only be cut in the village they were born. Angelone conveys the frustration of understanding and respecting beliefs. "Picture a situation where you would get a guy who fell off the damn mountain, cut his head. I could not cut his hair. I would have to part his hair the best I could and clean it. It was useless to suture the damn head…We would give them soap, keep it clean and have a delayed closure. But they would not let you cut that hair off, no way shape or form…"[178]

The Lao people's powerful belief in ghosts and spirits presented comical, though not at the time, scenes that are hard for the medic who witnessed them to believe, but happen they did. Angelone recalls coming upon a scene where a man was lying on the ground, trembling and shaking. A Lao soldier was leaning over the injured man spitting water all over his body and screaming in his ear as loud as he could. Angelone rushed up to help. He couldn't find a pulse and the soldiers blood pressure was "like 80 over nothing." Angelone got an IV going and opened it full blast, all the while, attempting to get the other men that had gathered around the scene away from the patient. Every time Angelone tried to put a blanket on the stricken man the other man would yank the blanket off of the injured man and continue to spit water on him. The interpreter kept telling Angelone to leave them alone. The interpreter told Angelone that he will tell the man spitting the water and screaming in the patients' ear that Angelone will bring the patient two chickens. At this point, thoroughly and utterly confused, Angelone agrees to bring the stricken man two chickens and some rice when they return to the camp. The interpreter relays this information to the 'screamer and spitter', who begins screaming in the mans ear once again, the patient becomes completely relaxed, stops shaking and comes out of shock. "What the hell happened?" Angelone asked. The interpreter explained to Angelone that the man had put himself into shock from being so scared he was unable to fulfill a promise he had made to his ghost. He had promised his ghost that if he got out of a firefight they had just been in, he would bring the ghost two chickens and some rice. Once the heat of battle subsided and the man found himself out in the middle of nowhere, in no position to buy chickens and rice to give to his ghost, he was terrified that since he had gone back on his promise his ghost would leave him eternally. The fervent belief that if your ghost leaves you, that's it, your soul will wander around forever. This man was literally in shock. Angelone believes the IV saved him, but this man was convinced that everything would be

OK once they returned to camp because the medic was going to get him some chickens and rice. Field expedient method or power of the human mind?[179]

> "A similar occurrence of self induced shock was observed by Angelone. This time, however, a primitive form of 'shock therapy' effected the psychiatric cure. The interpreter accompanying the medic proceeded to kick the victim in 'shock' until he came to. Whether or not medically sound, the results were highly effective."[180]

Understanding the attitudes and beliefs toward disease and medical treatment among the indigenous people is one of the most important skills the medic will acquire. Without that understanding, his job is almost impossible to perform. Even if he doesn't believe in it, it is vital that he convinces them that his medicine will work with theirs and it will be more effective because of their beliefs, not his. 'The method doesn't matter as long as the end results are the same' most aptly describes the philosophy that all medics practice. Western medicine and tribal rituals passed down through the centuries met and coexisted to compliment one another. Charging headlong into a world in which you knew very little about was a recipe for disaster that would not endear yourself to the local population.

The inhabitants of urban areas were somewhat more likely to seek the benefits of western medicine, than the remote hill tribes. However, traditions were difficult to overcome and it was not uncommon for the urban population to concur with both the western-trained doctors and the traditional herb doctors. Religious beliefs about death were vastly different than that of the westerner. Understanding the cultural differences and not attributing them to ignorance or comparing them to sub-standard measures is another facet of working in a culture that is completely foreign to everything you have been taught or accept as 'moral' or civilized.

Buddhist beliefs about life and death are quite a cultural shock to the westerner. Think for just a moment about the death of a baby. First, it is a child you don't know, but maybe just read about. Second, it is a child close to you. Think about what you are feeling about the loss of a young life. Now, try and imagine yourself thrust into a small village, thousands of miles away from home, the roads are dirty and dusty. The ramshackle buildings are made of scrounged materials of scrap wood, bamboo, thatch and rattan. Chickens, pigs and dogs are roaming about the streets among people you do not know and can barely converse with. This is what the medics were faced with. Angelone recalls a situation in which two world's mix.

> "I came out of my room, noticed a woman down on the street looking up at me. I nod, giving a greeting and go back in to wash up, shave and have breakfast. Coming downstairs to open my dispensary, she is the first one in the door. I noticed on the bench we had outside, she had a dead child.
>
> Angelone: "What is the matter?"
>
> Lao Lady: "The baby last night quit breathing."
>
> Angelone: "Why in hell didn't you come and get me when it was sick last night?"[181]

Angelone explains the mothers' behavior. "She didn't want to bother me. She felt she should not disturb me…I brought it back home and they cremated the kid. It was so weird. They had dogs all over town. This puppy came over to the hooch, she started feeding the puppy and the puppy stood there."[182] The interpreter later told Angelone that the mother had told him, "She was happy her daughter was so pleased in her home, that she came back."[183] Angelone was witnessing the belief in reincarnation, "Then I found out after these seven trips back (*Buddhist beliefs prescribes an individual receives seven lives*) you don't have to come back as a human, you can come back as an animal. As far as that woman was concerned, that puppy was her child. She believed that. Needless to say, that puppy got all it needed to eat, drink, etc."[184]

Beliefs and traditions varied from region to region in the country. There were underlying traditions with a common basis that attributed the cause of disease to either a "pathological, spirit (*called 'phi' in Lao, pronounced 'pea'*) intervention, sorcery and/or an imbalance among the thirty two souls (Kwan) that inhabit the body. Each of these 'Kwan' has a corresponding physical organ or intellectual faculty within the body. An absence or wandering of a specific soul created corresponding ailments."[185] Treatments for the resulting illness required that the appropriate ritual be performed by a Buddhist Monk to return the wandering soul to the body. Most often, the rituals consisted of the use of traditional herbal medicines that have been practiced for hundreds of years. The necessary rituals and ingredients for the potions included roots and powdered horns to be administered by the village spiritual leader, based upon the determined illness. The 'cure' would satisfy the souls in question.

There are multiple different belief variations of Buddhism that added complexity to the varied mix of people of Laos. Angelone described another belief he encountered which vividly depicts the powerful belief in Buddhism prevalent among the inhabitants of Laos.

> "If they had a big Buddhas, they could not get hurt. They all had this little green bag tied on their neck and they had these Buddhas in them. You can't just go out and buy a Buddha, a friend has to give it to you and given in a sincere manner. No harm would then come to them. What used to crack me up is the guy would get wounded and have a sack full of Buddhas around his neck. He would never, ever believe he had a bad Buddha! He would believe he did something wrong and the Buddha was punishing him. 'You did not do *this right!' so—bam!* 'You get wounded!' They had that much faith in that little green bag. They would do unbelievable things because they felt, 'I got a good Buddha and I am not going to get hurt.'"[186]

This type of belief was also seen time and again by Special Forces members working with Cambodian troops during the Vietnam War. Another lesson learned in Laos.

CHAPTER 17

FIELD EXPEDIENCY

Upon close observation, it becomes rapidly evident why Special Forces desired a creative thinking individual that could adapt to their surroundings and complete their mission. The basic nature of the medical training in and of itself did allow some degrees of success in training Laotian medics. Most of the training was procedural, not theoretical. The requirements for teaching the application of splints and field dressings could be accomplished by physically showing the procedure; thereby placing less emphasis on verbal communication. The abilities of the medic to adapt, improvise and acquire materials readily available to help impart, inspired many ingenious systems to counter the lack of supplies and communication difficulties. The medics still encountered difficulties when using interpreters to ascertain medical information from and relay instructions to patients. Obtaining a medical history was not in the realm of possibilities. The lack of laboratory confirmation left diagnostic determinations to be made through a single examination of the patient. The pictures, signs and symptoms of diseases they had seen and learned about during their training were the only thing the medics could use for comparison to determine a diagnosis.

This communication gap extended to the instructional training being provided for Laotian medics. This experience highlighted the need for medical kits containing learning aids for use in visual training to overcome the lack of conceptual abilities among people that had minimal exposure to western medicine. The indigenous people had a great deal of difficulty visualizing the simple examples of sanitation practices, such as the digging of latrines. To counter this impediment Ned Miller recalls that there was always a need to improvise. During his first tour in Laos north of Pakse at a Regional Training Center in a village named Pak Song, he conducted sick call prior to providing medical training scheduled for the Lao Army medics in the afternoon. There were only three interpreters available to the team. Some demolitions and weapons training were also scheduled for the same time as his medical training. The interpreter for his class was pulled to cover the other training needs. Miller recalls the awkward situation and how improvisation is a trademark of SF'ers and is euphemistically referred to as 'field expedient methods' to overcome any hindrance impeding the progress and success of the mission.

> "There I was with maybe those ten usable sentences! That was a challenge. I go ahead and I sketch and I draw. I drew a hillside, a guy up on the hillside shooting down in the valley. Then I'm showing a medic with an armband and him going in to get to the wounded guy out without him getting shot. One of the people in the class, a Lao, had been to Ft. Benning—so I made him interpreter! Boy, he started rattling on and from the pictures we got into all the carries and drags. It worked out really well."[187]

It is said that 'a picture is worth a thousand words' and the medics seized upon this through the use of any method of drawing they could devise in order to teach their lessons. Any method of drawing helped aid the medic in getting his lessons taught. By drawing a sequence of the procedure or concept being taught, trainees could more easily grasp the idea of how to perform a specific task. Using a stick in the dirt was the most readily available drawing resource. Some other clever substitutes included, Miller added, "A grease pencil could be used on a piece of paper that has been covered with combat acetate. If nothing else, you take a Safeway paper sack that can be cut out and opened to something like 2 foot by 3 foot, cover both sides with combat acetate, fold it up and put it in your pocket and have your grease pencil, you're in dog heaven!"[188] Miller wishes he still had some of those valuable pieces of artwork.

The poor health conditions, which existed among the Lao people, were mostly attributable to the lack of quality training for Lao medical personnel. Additionally, these very limited medical resources were stretched very thin, and in most cases, were non-existent among the remote and widely dispersed population. For those that had access to medical care, the medical standards and proficiency of the Laotian caregivers was woefully insufficient. The level of training and skill that the Special Forces medic possessed equaled and, in many cases, surpassed that of the medical professionals in Laos. A great deal of credit for the medics success in the field is due to the surgeons who assisted in preparing them prior to deployment. Their faith and confidence in the abilities of the men is proudly evident through Miller's recollections, "We had been trained in regular training and our pre-mission training, we had been run through the mill. We were pretty well ready for what came at us."[189] During Ned Miller's second deployment to Laos he recalled bearing witness to one of war's many horrible realities and illustrates why the SF medic requires such intense and extensive military and medical training. This is just one, among thousands of experiences, reflecting why the Special Forces medics' had to possess the maturity and skills to handle the responsibilities they encountered in Laos.

> "Late one rainy, mean, miserable night, a runner came from the Group Colonel [Laotian] wanting to know if I would go up to the medical section and give them some help. Their doctor had gone to someplace to get medical supplies and they had several casualties. I actually was put in the position where I filled in for the Group Surgeon (Lao). That night, that was quite a challenge. I found out that most of our training had brought us right up to that level with no problem. You quickly remember that you're not God. Even if you're a full-trained American doctor—you realize you're not God. There were some things you just could not fix. Some of them were already dead, some

> you could stop the bleeding, tie off the bleeders and keep 'em alive to be evacuated. From up in the jungle they were evacuated down to the Nam Tha Regional Headquarters and then put on an airplane, which would be Air America, or a Royal Lao airplane. Then down to Luang Prabang or Vientiane."[190]

The problems encountered by the medics associated with language barriers and a high illiteracy rate require close examination to convey the SF medics' endless resourcefulness to achieve their objective. Fred Hardy's experiences are illustrative of the medics' ability to adapt and just do what needed to get done.

> "I was supposed to end up going to open a refugee camp with the Meo tribesman. We proceeded to get the equipment in the helicopter and I was supposed to have an interpreter. That morning, everyone was there but the interpreter. They said, 'Go ahead Fred, the interpreter will be up on the next helicopter.' The next helicopter that came up was the exact one for the way back when that tour was over. So I went up in this strange place with no interpreter."[191]

Hardy found himself among 300 refugees, in a valley near the plains of the Bolovens Plateau, at a place called Yat Moot. Here he was, without an interpreter and only six weeks of language training during pre mission training, which was of some help, but the Hmong tribe had its own dialect and no written language. Well, there was no sense in complaining he had a job to do. With the help of the people he had come to help, they erected the tents and he completed setting up his medical equipment in time to begin seeing patients the following morning.

Prescribing medications, a seemingly simple procedure, presented a need to think unconventionally. Most Lao people did not understand the concept of taking pills every so many hours to cure an illness. Medics often experienced that passing out pills to the villagers to be taken at a later time, was often a problem. Sometimes the villagers sold them or took more than the prescribed amount based upon the principle; "if two pills make me feel good, any number of additional pills are bound to make me feel that much better."[192] The people had no concept of an overdose; it just did not exist in their mind. This potential danger required unique yet simple solutions. Hardy remembered his first day of business in the refugee camp.

> "The first morning I learned well that whatever pill I had on the table, that was the most colorful, I started getting the same symptoms from everyone in line. So, I decided what they wanted was the most colorful pill. After that, I moved back in the tent and started them coming in one at a time."[193]

After a month to six weeks had passed, Hardy had the language down to a crude level of communication. Between using the 'round robin' interpreter system and his 'mastery' of the language, he could determine what a villager's ailment was. Occasionally, gestures and pointing to the area that hurt provided a sufficient means of communicating ailments—headache, stomach ache, chest pain, etc. Hardy said it was a "very symptomatic type treatment. If he had a stomach ache with diarrhea, or he had a stomach ache without diarrhea...after awhile you could almost figure it was worms or some kind of intestinal parasite"[194] The prevalent medicine used for this malady was *hexylresorcinol*, for adults, and *piperazine* (both were common medications to treat worm infestations) for the children. Teaching the villagers not to chew or take all of the medicine at once required similar simple solutions. The most common method employed was to have them return for the next dose a few times and make sure they learn to not chew or consume all of the medicine dispensed at once. Once this instruction was imparted with reasonable success, they could be sent home with a day's worth to take on their own.

The local Shaman actually inadvertently helped diagnose some cases. He would come and sit in the dispensary, watching over Hardy. Hardy felt that the witch doctor came there because Hardy represented a threat to his standing among the tribesmen, kind of "stealing his thunder."[195] Hardy recalls the shaman had a glass tube that was heated up and applied to the ill patient's body wherever he hurt, to suck out the evil spirits. This 'treatment' left a burn mark about the size of a half-dollar. This inadvertently helped Hardy determine an individual problem during sick call. "When a guy came in with a burn on his forehead, he had a headache and I gave them aspirin. If he had the mark on his chest, I listen to his chest, he probably has a cold."[196] In this fashion, the basic medical aches, pains and discomforts could be relieved. Two benefits came from not having the witch doctor stop this practice; Hardy was able to determine the general area of need without conversing and the shaman maintained his status with the people by getting credit for his 'suction cup' treatment removing the spirit causing the illness.

The medics' often relied upon symbols and other visual aids to communicate directions and convey concepts for which the villagers had little comprehension. The use of mimicking actions was a common language tool employed to get a point across to the diverse cultures. "They watch you, what you do and this is the way they learn."[197], said Wyngaert. Wyngaert also recalled the challenge of teaching patients how to take prescribed medicines in specified doses and according to specific timelines. The people did not understand clocks and time. However, they did understand differences in the day. The sun rising, the sun all the way up and the sun setting. That is how the medic taught them to take pills. "The way you have to explain it to them is the sun comes up, you take a pill. When the sun is all the way overhead, you take a pill. When the sun goes down, you take a pill. Pointing at the medicine, this is your medicine, you take it three times a day."[198] Wyngaert also found out very quickly that it was hard to make them understand that if by giving them a little was good for them didn't necessarily mean, "a whole lot will be real good. If you gave them medicine, say for a week to ten days, they used to take it all in three days! I used to give them enough for two days and have them come back. Otherwise, they would take it all at one time, if you didn't watch them."[199]

The possibility of villagers accidentally switching and mixing the uses and directions for medicine added yet another level of complexity. The medics found this situation could be resolved with artistic skills and portioning of medications. Angelone once had a woman come in with her daughter who was covered with sores, and the mother complained that she herself had diarrhea. Angelone treated the mother with *tetracycline*, a broad spectrum anti-biotic, and cleaned the little girls' sores with a scrub brush and *phisohex*, a soap-less skin cleansing disinfectant. Before leaving, he instructed the mother on the proper use and care of the child's sores by using the brush and phisohex and prescribed Kaopectate for the mother's diarrhea. The next day, the mother was carried into the dispensary, doubled over and vomiting. After a while, it was determined that she had applied the Kaopectate to the girl's sores and taken the phisohex. Angelone continues, "How do you combat that? If we had two medicines like that, that were the same color, in the same size bottle we would put it in regular prescription bottles. Then we would draw a little child on the bottle and relay that this one is for the child. An adult woman, represented by drawing a breast on the person, was drawn on the other one."[200]

The 'virgin' patients, people that have never been subjected to western medicine, presented further concerns based upon no previous exposure to most medicines being prescribed and any possible resulting allergic reactions. The medics had to operate under the assumption that there would be a good and favorable result from the medicines they were dispensing. If the patient suffered ill effects, they must be prepared to react quickly. Angelone once treated a case of *anaphylactic shock*, which is a serious and often life threatening allergic reaction characterized by low blood pressure, shock and difficulty breathing. This occurred after he injected some Triasin B into a patient suffering a deficiency caused by the polished rice supplied by the US.

> "Boy it looked bad. We would give them Triasin B every 24 hours and then a handful of Vitamin B tablets. This one guy came in and I hit him with Triasin B and he got as far as outside and—*bam*! He fell and turned as red as a cherry, got real warm. I gave him some epinephrine, a cc of cortisone and got him to Doc Meni."[201]

CHAPTER 18

DOC, IN ANY LANGUAGE

The indomitable spirit driven by the Special Forces medics' compassion and sense of responsibility for the health and welfare of his team and the people they are there to assist manifests itself in a mindset which can be likened to that of a mother bear, sensitive, caring and fiercely protective.

In Laos, for example, the harsh conditions in the strange and hostile land required a special drive, typical of SF medics, to solve problems that were seriously affecting the health the Laotian. FTT 11-A, a six man split detachment arrived at a Royal Laotian Battalion Headquarters during the monsoon season of October 1961. Stationed high atop a mountain peak, thirty-five miles north of Paksane, they found a scene that conjured a feeling of traveling back in time. Most of the Lao soldiers appeared to be longhaired boys. The team later discovered that cutting their hair outside of their native village was taboo. This helped identify how long an individual had been out in the jungle, and from the appearance of the battalion members, they had been in the bush for a long time. FTT 11-A's tactical training mission was to advise the Royal Laotian soldiers, 650 strong, to hold a position in the mountain valley and contain any Pathet Lao forces attempting to enter Paksane.

Special Forces medic, Sergeant Charles 'Huk' Heaukulani immediately went to work assessing the medical situation and health of the Lao troops. Through the jungle, he followed the Laotian medics he was now charged with to an outpost, where he found a horrific mess. Approximately forty men were scattered about the camp with their bellies bloated. Six men a day were dying and no one knew why. While he was checking temperatures, pulses, blood pressures and investigating the color of their skin—two more men died. Back in camp for the night with his team, he just couldn't figure out what was wrong. The morning light brought further bad news from out of the jungle encampment, more men had died. Grabbing his medical bag, he set off for what must have appeared to be a camp with an epidemic. He was determined to do his best to determine the cause of the illness and hopefully save the lives of the Lao soldiers still alive. Later that day, he came back to the team camp to get some supplies and returned to the outpost before nightfall. His frustration was evident to his team members. "I have one that is about dead right now. I've got to go back and help as much as I can. I'd really like to know what's killing so many."[202] Huk spent the night with the sick Laotians, desperately seeking an answer. SP5 Bobby Gregory, team demo man, returned to the team after spending the better part of the day helping Huk. The outlook was grim.

Huk's desire to help overpowered the exhausting events of the past forty-eight hours, twenty-four of them with no sleep, 'Huk' reported another man had died during the night, when he returned to camp for some food and his medical books. His dedication and training finally bore results, "It's the simplest god damn thing!"[203] He almost shouted with excitement. "They're not getting any Vitamin B!"[204] After speaking with the Lao soldiers in the camp and still being unable to determine the cause or the illness, he began to look through the *Merck Manual* and started searching the symptom section. A reference to Orientals and Asians getting *beri beri* had caught his eye. The Laotians should have been getting enough of the vitamin through their steady diet of rice. The problem was right in front of him—big bags of rice marked 'U.S.'—that was it! The people were not eating *their* rice. Rice from the United States is polished…no husks. The Laotians were eating the American rice that had no source of Vitamin B. Their diet wasn't balanced. Besides the rice, the Americans had additional food sources in addition to the rice that provided a balance of vitamins. Now that he had determined the cause, he had to rely on an inventive solution to provide a cure. There was no injectable Vitamin B available, only pills. The sick Laotians could not hold anything down. One 'field expedient method,' coming up! The pills would have to be used as suppositories. The alternative was to lose another fast fading patient. The body only absorbs about 25% of the dosage in this manner. He literally pumped the sick man full of pills. A drastic and dramatic change occurred, the man's blood pressure and temperature came down. Soon, he was able to drink and hold down water. Huk exclaimed jubilantly, "I started on the other twenty men, and for a twenty-four hour period no one died. NO ONE FUCKING DIED!"[205] His undying dedication and determination is a representative trait that all medics must possess.

It is ironic that the very food sent to help the Laotian people by the US government, as part of its attempts to encourage them to resist communist subversion, made them sick and provided the medic an opportunity to win their trust and friendship. It is a good example of the preemptive measures Special Forces medics conducted to counter potential propaganda used by the Pathet Lao. Had the Pathet Lao been in the position, it is probable that they would have blamed the food sent by the 'imperialists" as poisoning the people. 'Huk' had saved the lives of sixty Laotians and his findings were reported to 'WHITE STAR' Headquarters. Unknown at the time, Laotians in other areas were dying of the same symptoms. Soon, all team medics were administering Vitamin B shots, in addition to having the Lao troops mix fish oil with their rice. It was a rocky start, and the prognosis was difficult, but the perseverance of a well-trained physician substitute, the Special Forces medic, had won the battle. Huk continued to build on that hard won foundation by traveling to outlying posts and villages, making sure that the people were following the prescribed cure in an attempt to minimize the intestinal illnesses prevalent at sick call. His team leader described the care and concern his medic displayed for the team and the people of Laos. "Huk was like a mother hen to us, pushing vitamins, quinine and antibiotics. He would get really upset when we wouldn't take our daily doses. That's what he was there to do, for us and the Lao."[206]

Another example of the medics' desire to help those around them under the harshest of conditions was that of Fred Hardy. Hardy recalls, during his stay at the refuge camp, that during the day he felt relatively at ease, in spite of the strange surroundings and language barrier, while conducting sick call and dispensing medicine. The nights were completely different. There he was, stuck out in the middle of the jungle in a strange land, with no companion. There was nobody he could talk with. The morning light could not come soon enough. He remembers one night specifically, where the feeling of vulnerability struck especially hard. Some tribesmen had come to get him in the middle of the night. It took some time, to determine through gestures and the convoluted process of interpretation, for him to understand what the problem was. A man was having trouble breathing. He grabbed his tracheotomy kit and a few other items to head out into the night, to a nearby village.

> "We had practiced [tracheotomies], but I had never done it on a person, at night, with no assistance and a little flashlight. I got all this together and thought to myself, 'Hey! If this guy dies, I am all alone. What is going to happen to me?' I really had no idea what to do. For some reason I took a syringe and put some epinephrine (a synthetic adrenaline) in it and went up the hill. When we got there, the guy was laying on the floor, very difficult breathing, but breathing, like an asthma attack. The witch doctor was sitting on a chair sprinkling beads of water on his forehead."[207]

Hardy was faced with one of the tenuous situations that medics were trained for and warned about. A tracheotomy, even performed by a doctor under the best conditions, is a skilled procedure. An illness such as this one was pretty severe and found the shaman in a position of not knowing what exactly could be done. His call for the American medic, the man who was, 'stealing his thunder', to help was a last resort. The maturity and the training of a medic were put to test in such situations. Hardy had never heard of anyone having an asthma attack in the area. It was purely an assumption, based on the diagnosis of symptoms he had learned during training. It was a very dramatic scene, to say the least… unable to talk with the patient, having no medical history to refer too and, alone with no outside support. If he succeeded in helping the man, it would be a major victory and a success in gaining the confidence of the people. If he failed, one could only guess. Hardy began to inject the syringe he had filled with epinephrine. By the time he was removing the needle, the man had started breathing easier. "I had made a lot of points in that area."[208] From that time on, everyone in that village called him 'Tan Maw', Doctor in Laotian. By practicing what he had learned and not attempting the more difficult treatment method first, Hardy had won over the respect and the trust of the village and kept in line with the medics' creed, 'Do No Harm'.

These instances provide a strong testament in which the medics initiative and compassion are recognized as an effective tool for the success of the overall team mission.

CHAPTER 19

LESSONS LEARNED

Laos presented a live training environment for SF missions to come in Vietnam. The counter-insurgency role was rapidly developing and Special Forces received on the job training throughout the country. For the medic, he was going in almost blind, the pre-mission training he received prepared him well for dealing with the conventional Special Forces doctrine, of operating in occupied Europe, but Southeast Asia was an entirely different realm. "The lack of up to date medical data and tropical experience, coupled with the expected brevity of the mission, few clues were available as to the nature and extent of the medical problems they would have to contend with."[209] Teams going to Laos during HOTFOOT experienced a higher degree of 'going in blind' because they were the first teams deploying to the area and had no previous experiences to draw upon. Miller explains how the teams had little to no chance to exchange information with teams relieving each other,

> "Sometimes the plane that brought in the new team was the same plane taking the old one back out. So you had those very few minutes you were being unloaded and they were putting their stuff on, and that was all the time you had, and that was not good. They finally learned that whenever possible, if you were earmarked for a certain location you might be able to contact the team leader of who had this place and you could actually get communications going between you and them. I don't know if this happened very many times it was a possibil-

ity to get a radio relay going. We had no idea who had been there before us until we got there."[210]

The 'HOTFOOT' and 'WHITE STAR' operations thrust Special Forces teams into an environment that varied drastically throughout Laos. Incidentally, this provided the opportunity for Special Forces to further develop their tactics in guerrilla warfare for eventual implementation in Vietnam. Ned Miller attested to the invaluable experiences. "It was unintentional, but it just happened that way. Laos got us ready for Vietnam. We learned so many lessons in Laos that made things possible in Vietnam. Our people were tired old warriors by the time they got over to Vietnam."[211]

The most significant change to the medics' role was that of the medical civic action programs (MEDCAP). Prior to involvement in Laos there was not a clear mandate or focus for such projects. However, based upon feedback from returning teams describing the benefits of alleviating illness and disease at the village level a 7th Group Headquarters directive was issued in April 1961 encouraging the activity through a variety of civic action programs. Prior to Special Forces departure from Laos in August 1962, medical benefits reached about 19,000 people. It proved to be an effective tool to combating Pathet Lao efforts to gain the allegiance of the local population. The villagers who once viewed the medics and the strange medicine they had brought, with fear and skepticism, now came to them as friends and trusted healers. This elevated status among the villagers often led to some bizarre situations. Angelone once had a villager come by canoe to get him. Angelone, who assumed there was an injured person in need of assistance at the village, where Angelone finally got a good glimpse of his 'patient'. After a four-hour trip up the river, "It was a water buffalo! Their tractor. I showed him how to clean it (the wound) out and keep it clean."[212] The villager insisted that he sew up the wound. "Have you ever tried to suture a water buffalo? I didn't know if I had sutures big enough. The damn water buffalo, you don't tell a water buffalo to not lay in the mud! I did not put that many sutures in him, a couple, just to show him I was doing it."[213] Winning the hearts and the minds!

The old adage, 'A pound of prevention', was most often the medics' guiding principle when implementing health programs. By reducing the potential for disease the villagers health would improve. It was also something that the villagers themselves could continue to practice once Special Forces left the area, thereby reducing the reliance on outside assistance. Sanitation efforts presented the best opportunities for positive results. Villagers were encouraged to pick up refuse, cut grass and remove debris and undergrowth from underneath their homes. Village authorities were enlisted to implement programs that would control homeless, vicious packs of dogs that contributed to the spread of disease and the potential to cause serious injuries among the villagers. Herbicide and pesticide spraying programs were developed with specific villagers trained in the mixing and application of the chemicals. Programs such as these were intended to reduce the disease carrying rat population by destroying their habitat. Drainage projects were designed to eradicate breeding areas for the abundant mosquitoes, combined with chloroquine programs to control the ever-present malaria. A preventive measure for disease spreading flies was quite simple—fly swatters were distributed! Latrines were dug and drinking water wells were established. Variations of MEDCAP had been conducted for years wherever medics were operating, but the programs in Laos were the training-ground for the preventive medicine programs that would become standard operating procedure among Special Forces medics.

One of the most important lessons learned in Laos was the absolutely essential need to understand the local culture of inhabitants in an operational area. The ability to understand the people the medic was to work with became a focused topic of instruction added to the medical training regimen in the U.S. Many of the medics driven by their own interest and initiative, accompanied roving medical patrols conducted by non-military U.S. agencies that provided basic medical treatment, malaria control and sanitation projects throughout the Laotian countryside.

'After Action Reports' (AAR) from returning teams provided valuable information about the people and how to approach them, and names and locations of where they could get medical help if needed, such as the 7th Day Adventist Hospital. Angelone recalls that "All this stuff was a tremendous help."[214] Implementation of successful medical programs always encountered difficulties, but the experience and intelligence gathered and relayed to incoming teams through AAR's increased the degree of success of programs by reducing cultural misunderstandings.

Perhaps the most difficult cultural misunderstanding encountered by medics was the positional relation and importance of the local shaman in village society. It became easier, at least mentally, to confront and address the differences with the local shaman, or whatever person that passed as the local healer through an increased awareness of their importance in society. The local healers used a mixture of rituals, folk medicine, black magic and sorcery to care for his charges. In the remotest regions, the shamans' undoubtedly felt that their social status was threatened by western medicine. It was absolutely essential that the medic gain the trust and cooperation of this person, to assure the teams success, who generally held a very high place of importance within the village.

Medics deployed found that "primitive medical practices throughout the country were more the rule than the exception. The village sorcerers and practitioners were a powerful force to cope with when up-to-date medical practices were introduced."[215] Sometimes, sorcerers attempted to undermine the medic and his medicine by referring the more difficult cases of illness or injury to them. By not participating in the healing process, the sorcerer was taking a calculated risk that if the medics' efforts failed his credibility would be damaged among the villagers thus strengthening the sorcerers, based on an ineffective treatment. Often, neither the shaman nor the medic would likely have been successful due to the severity of the case.

The medic had to be capable of making a mature decision based on his training, react accordingly. For example, Ned Miller recalls an occasion, on his first deployment during June 6, 1960 to December 3, 1960 with FTT-47, when villagers of a little Hmong village just north of Nam Tha requested his assistance. The villagers were in desperate need of medical care. The only medical care available was provided by the village shaman.

> "They had someone very sick and they had sent someone down asking for help. We fought our way up the mountainside in one of our jeeps, very rough road, got up there, and no question about it—roaring case of appendicitis. You ask yourself, 'do I do a abdominal surgery in this setting right here or do we take a chance on massive dosages of antibiotics?' I got a better chance of going antibiotics. The witch doctor is right there working on this guy. He's got his little mask on, his chicken bones and everything else. He's chanting, 'Ahhh, woo, woo, woo…' the whole bit. I went ahead and gave an injection of penicillin. Went ahead and run sick call for the entire village while I was up there. Checked in on our patient before we left on back down the mountain—witchdoctor was still working out. The next day we started back up there and those people had come out there and rebuilt that road! Not wide, but it was as smooth as a tabletop. We got up there and they had built us a two-room dispensary. The witchdoctor was still there working out but not as fervent, because *our* patient was sitting up. That witch doctor had earned his money. Now, the idea there I've heard of some people—actually would work it out so a witch doctor would be their assistant in a sick call. They get the credit for all of the good anyway. But, in that case, he got as much credit as my little injection of a couple million units of penicillin. I was very impressed with his efforts."[216]

The shaman practicing ancient tribal methods, in addition to what Miller did, was just that much better as far as the patient, the shaman and the inhabitants of the village were concerned.

The remote regions in which medics operate place a great deal of pressure upon the medic. This is due in part, to the unavailability of air evacuation of a seriously ill or wounded patient. Effective, quantifiable results dictated mission success or failure. The entire team mission could be compromised if treatment was not effective.

Angelone recalled a scenario in which he thought his treatment had failed.

> "I had this one woman in the village, the largest village [along the Nam Son River]. It was weird, she had a fever of 104–105, one breast was as hard as a rock. She just had a two-week old baby. We really did not know what to do with her so I got on the 'horn' and called back. I got Dr. Meni on the radio, who was a Thai doctor, they had a surgical unit there. When he told me what to do, he said 'look, don't try to cut into her, try her on massive antibiotics.' I gave her antibiotics and stayed with her about two days. The fever broke and the breast started softening up. To this day I don't know what she had but the breast started softening up and the fever broke. One breast, it was as hard as a table, there were no lumps, just the whole breast was hard. After a couple days I came back and went out to follow up. When I got over there it scared the hell out of me. When I walked up the stairs, she was laying down and had this veil in front of her and this monk was there and gave her a bowl of rice and an orange stick and an egg in it. This guy had a bamboo flute playing. 'Oh my God, I killed her.' I thought she was dead, they said to come on in. Then, I saw her moving! We just sat there; after it was all over they thanked me and said 'Well, she is cured'. The Monk was just thanking Buddha, I almost died, I thought that woman died on me. In that village, from then on, every time I went over there the kids came out to meet me and everyone who had any kind of ailment would come to me."[217]

There was one medical procedure in which the medics were consistently warned to not involve themselves unless it was of absolute necessity. Childbirth. Getting involved, other than in an assisting role with the process of childbirth, was strongly discouraged during a medic's training. They were, however, encouraged to stay and keep an eye on the baby's health and welfare. Dr. Meni, also suggested the same to Angelone while operating from an area known as Pad 9, which was basically a valley that led into Paksane. The team was there for about nine weeks as a blocking force to guard against the Pathet Lao entering the town. Angelone had a few occasions where he stayed and observed a few births performed by the midwives trained at Dr. Meni's Hospital. He recalls Dr. Meni advising that, "If the child is having difficulty, give it some supportive treatment, clear the nasal passage, clear its throat, get him going with mouth to mouth if you have to."[218] Angelone was very fortunate in that he was only a radio call away from a medical doctor, as a backup for problems he was unable to handle. "A lot of medics I talked to came back and never saw a doctor."[219] He relied heavily on Dr. Meni and realized how lucky he was to have his support and the option to bring a tough case, like a woman who had a miscarriage and was hemorrhaging, back to his hospital. "I will tell you now, in 85% of your births, the woman can handle [it] by herself anyway."[220]

Volumes of medical information resulted from Special Forces deployment in Laos. The health condition of the average Laotian was comparable to any other population of an under-developed country. Their average life expectancy of thirty-five years (1971 figures) and a high infant mortality rate were a direct result of the tropical diseases and illness' prevalent in a country with a poor diet and exposure to multiple mosquito transmitted diseases. The cool climate of the highlands and the mountains are prime conditions that foster a large number of respiratory diseases.

> "The incidence of disease is made worse in Laos by a climate that favors the survival of insects and other disease vectors outside the human body. Mosquitoes are abundant the year round, and the innumerable mosquito breeding places in the forests, rice paddies and watercourses challenge even the most extensive control measures. Flies of various kinds, lice, fleas and

> mites—all disease carriers—thrive in the environment. Because of inadequacies in the normal diet, there is malnutrition among all age groups, which accounts for dietary deficiency diseases and for a lowering of resistance to infection."[221]

Sanitation and water contamination presented a problem of magnitude, incomprehensible to the civilized westerner. All of these conditions coupled with primitive medical practices lead to widespread, in some cases epidemics, of *cholera*, *scrub typhus*, *tuberculosis*, *trachoma* and a myriad of intestinal infestations leading, most often than not, to hepatitis. Other diseases, such as smallpox, typhoid, multiple venereal diseases and dermatological problems, were the norm, rather than the exception. The medics were able to diagnose the illness and could prescribe the needed medication to heal the condition, but their job was to also educate the people in order to create and maintain a living environment that minimized the illness' occurrence. Preventive medicine was the best medicine and with that in mind, the medics taught the villagers proper human waste disposal practices, such as not relieving themselves in the open areas of their village or in the water source they used for cooking and bathing. Food preparation and storage methods were extremely unsanitary; consumption of meat not preserved was a major contributing cause of most intestinal infestations.

Any medic serving in Laos, when asked, what was the most difficult task or situation they encountered, stated that it was not the weather, terrain, animals and insects of the jungle. It was difficulty convincing the people that the most important aspect of medicine was sanitation. Difficulty in conveying the importance that preventive measures for treating and limiting the instances of the most basic ailments the human can suffer, presented itself and time and time again to the SF medic.

> "As far as compassion for the sick and wounded was concerned, the Lao had little in common with their advisors. There was a distinct disregard for even the most rudimentary elements of sanitation by western standards. Latrines were initially considered frills and many indigenous units had the habit

> of relieving themselves in the immediate vicinity or periphery of the encampments. What seemed to keep the possibility of disease under control was the frequent relocation of such military encampments. Commanders were mostly disinterested in sanitation problems for their own sake. For the Special Forces medic it was often difficult to impress local units with the importance of sanitation."[222]

There were many logistical and technical aspects that received further operational considerations because of the lessons learned in Laos. The scarcity of support services such as better equipped medical facilities and inconsistent supply methods added to the isolation of the teams. Miller recalls that there were no American doctors, other than Dr. Tom Dooley, in the Nam Tha area. Some French doctors had opened practices in towns, but the small villages did not have any access to medical care.

The medical re-supply system also left much to be desired. There was virtually no viable distribution system and the constant shortage of supplies seriously hampered FAR training operations. SFC Alan Maggio with FTT-45 (March 1962 to September 1962) recalls having to wait for supplies before training could begin. The teams deployed with their own medical supplies, but once expendables such as medicine and bandaging, were used, the time lag between re-supply was, at times, ridiculous. Sometimes a team's requisitioned supplies did not arrive until after their departure and after a new team had replaced them. There was also an inherent reluctance by some U.S. Agencies to part with medical supplies. Dr. Radcliffe recalls that the

> "Lack of medical expendables was a constant headache after we consumed the drugs and supplies we physically carried with us. Our covert quasi-civilian status compounded the problems, as American advisers. Medical administration refused us access to supplies which were destined for the Laotians whether they were being used or not."[223]

Later operations had this problem addressed by the use of Filipino technical advisors, who guarded several depots that would receive, store and distribute supplies ordered from the United States by the American advisors. This helped offset the supply problem, but the ever present profiteering by the selling of medical supplies on the black market and the dependence the Lao acquired from the US supply system created an unwanted disregard to establishing, improving and operating a sufficient Lao system.

Laotian operations also highlighted the lack of and/or the impracticality of some supplies for use in the guerrilla warfare environment. Changes were necessary to meet the need of teams operating in a tropical, hot and humid climate where size and wieght of equipment played an important part of a teams mobility. The development of the portable field laboratory, escape and evasion kits, emergency medical kits and individual medical packets containing iodine, morphine and anti-malarial medicines all had their origins in Laos.

Another important component of Special Forces medical operations was the continued support Special Forces doctors and surgeons provided for deployed medics. This emphasized and recognized the necessity to support the detachment medics in an operational area. The surgeon accompanying the first deployment of WHITE STAR medics, Dr. William B. Radcliffe, (November 1960 tho May 1961) recalled some instances requiring an ability of surgeons to employ 'field expedient' solutions to accomplish the mission, medical and non-medical, they provided Special Forces medics in Laos.

> "It was my job to see that requests for medical supplies were filled—I actually set up a stockroom and packaged and shipped these myself. Next, I would advise on problems. A sick team member might need a closer look, such as *refractory diarrhea* or *amebic colitis.* Evacuation when required was to an American missionary hospital in Bangkok. On occasion civilians with complex problems were evacuated and referred to a Philippine run hospital in Vientiane. I visited every team at

> least once, and was able to advise and consult on any problem that had come up. Additional examples: one aidman galvanized local officials into constructing a town dispensary or health center and they needed paint. After visiting the site I was able to coax a couple of gallons of paint out of the local AID officials. On another occasion a medic undertook a wide scale *malaria prophylaxis* program with a provincial chief who had heretofore been disinclined to talk to Americans at all, and I was able to come up with the necessary *chloroquine*. Finally, there were some odd jobs that were appropriate to a physician. We organized physical examinations for a newly recruited Laotian unit, which was being rushed to the north after an abbreviated training cycle. We eliminated those with gross physical disabilities, and incidentally discovered a 20 percent incidence of *palpable splenomegaly*."[224]

The medical intelligence gathered from Laotian operations indicated that diagnostic, pediatric, geriatric and area specific training required development or upgrading. Seemingly small and obvious diagnostic procedures initially presented treatment problems. Medics returning from Laos reported that when Western medicine was introduced into the unexposed Lao society, satisfactory results were derived from reduced dosages. This happened because the much smaller statured Lao villagers had no immunologic buildup to the drugs like the average sized American suffering the same symptoms. The drugs that the medics carried also had a predetermined dosage based on the average age of an individual. Age determination was extremely difficult because the physical make up of the Lao people was generally much smaller than that of their western counter-part. Therefore, it was realized, a reduced dosage rate for the medications was needed.

Another prevalent medical concern present in under developed countries, reinforced through medical experiences in Laos, is dental hygiene. Actually, it is the lack there of, that existed among the people. The medics had limited exposure to dental practices during training. In an operational setting, equipment availability and the impracticality of follow up treatment negated the use of temporary fillings. Emergency extractions were performed, when indicated by advanced decay after treatment for infection and swelling. "All I did was extract, I would not try to do any fillings. I don't know how to fill a tooth,"[225] Angelone recalls filling an APC (Aspirin, phenocetin and caffeine) bottle with pulled teeth. APC pills were once the military equivalent of Excedrin. Medic, Al Gunn remarked, "It was so widely used in the military that it acquired the slang term. 'All Purpose Capsule.'"[226] The containers, made of both glass and plastic, came in several sizes ranging from an average sized bottle holding 100 or so pills, to a quart sized container holding as much as 1,000 pills. The larger containers were most often used around the dispensary for holding multiple small items—extracted teeth are but one such example for it's use as a receptacle.

The information on diseases, injuries and cultural differences of this foreign environment filtered back to Ft. Bragg via returning teams, who were also examined and treated for diseases they may have been exposed to and could be carrying. Medical debriefings provided the impetus for a change in medical training procedures and topics from which both military and civilian medical institutions benefited. Ned Miller remembers that,

> "When we got back to the States, the doctors would really pump us because we had seen diseases first hand that they had only read about. I imagine these doctors were in related fields, from larger institutions. They had certain portions that were very interested in our type of work. They hadn't developed the present day EMT (Emergency Medical Technician). They had ambulance crews, but they didn't have that back then. They didn't have the super-trained people. A lot of people just hadn't been thrown into that type of situation—who had been asleep back here in the States. A lot of study and interest that went into this, back before Vietnam was a big issue. We had four hundred people committed on the ground in Laos."[227]

Subsequent debriefings of medics returning from Laos revealed diseases and illnesses encountered. For example, a common affliction that wreaked havoc among the inhabitants of Laos, and can be easily prevented, was Amebic Colitis. Most often referred to as Amebic Dysentery, is an inflammation of the colon, caused by the one-celled amoebas. It is usually acquired by ingesting food or water, which has been contaminated with feces. Associated symptoms of profuse diarrhea, abdominal pains and weight loss often seriously affect infants, elderly and debilitated people. Other potentially devastating illnesses such as *Palpable Splenomegaly*, an enlarged spleen that can be felt in the upper left portion of the abdomen, *monoclulsis*, *syphilis*, *tuberculosis* and *Hepatitis B* or *C* are indicative of the multiple contributing factors whose origins are most often found in unsanitary environments. A high rate of chronic exposure to malaria in underdeveloped countries is also a leading cause for many of the illnesses encountered. Malarial vectors, such as mosquitoes, carry the illnesses from host to host. The resulting malaria further weakens the infected person's immune system, creating ideal conditions for bacterial pathogens to develop. The discoveries, observations, and documentation of such high rates of these types of illnesses provided considerable indications that training be adjusted to enhance future medics knowledge, awareness and ability to recognize, prevent and treat these potentially life threatening problems.

Don Dougan's tour in Laos (January 1962 to September 1962) with FTT 7 at the Lao Officer Academy in Dong Hene provided lessons learned which he benefited from as a medical instructor with Training Group, service inVietnam and his eventual return to Laos. FTT-7 was tasked to train Laotian Officers in reconnaissance and ambush techniques. Once training was completed, the officers, accompanied by SF personnel, were taken out to the Tchepone area, for reconnaissance missions along the growing Ho Chi Minh Trail. This is where Highway 9 heads east into the Khe Sanh South Vietnam. The Lao officers did not receive any medical instruction. However, a dispensary operated by Sergeant First Class Elmo Clark was used for training Lao medics and the treatment of local villagers and troops. "The two biggest medical problems we had were hepatitis and skin infections. We used a hepatitis vaccine that had been developed by U.S. medical people to start an immunization program. For skin infections of our own people, where it was especially bad around the crotch area, we would put them in a room naked, turn on a big fan, it healed it faster than anything I know. All the god damn tropical ointment didn't do shit. Two or three days and they would be fine. Hey, it worked!"[228] Like most all other medics in Laos, he too, witnessed the animistic beliefs that would preclude such things as the building of dispensaries in certain areas because of trees and bushes holding some spiritual power. "The medic always practiced in conjunction with the local medicine man. They would sprinkle water all over the place. You just tolerated it, if you didn't, they would throw you out of there. You just went along with it."[229]

Finally, of the lessons learned, the demands placed upon the meager resources of manpower Special Forces could provide brought much needed support from higher echelons of command. The exhausting schedule of deployments created incredible pressures on the physical and psychological capabilities of the men and their families. The six-month rotational system was devised to promote stable family life, as much as possible. It was believed that the short TDY would offset the problems that arose from an extended deployment of these men, who were considerably older than the average regular Army soldiers and had families.

Ned Miller, who served two tours in Laos, the first being June 1960 to December 1960 and the other from February 1962 to September 1962. Miller, during a candid interview, provides some personal insight about the demands placed on active duty personnel.[230]

> "Let me rip this on you. We were also [beginning], starting in about '61 and '62, what was Kennedy's build up. They were gonna build Special Forces up to 10,000 people. It took some more of our people to conduct that training. In the meantime, teams that were going just kept going. There were some people; in five years were only home ten months. There was no end to

> it; the majority of people going had been on that mission before or other missions before that. They were fully qualified veterans. Good, solid people. You look at how many people went back for seconds. Worldwide, we only had about 2,500 people and the people were on the go continuously. They were rode hard and put up wet. They had no time, no family time. That really didn't work, you went right back into mission training, classroom, night maneuvers at Camp Mackall, the swamps in Georgia…you're always somewhere else."[231]

Miller provided a vivid picture of the tremendous demand for operational teams. In a five-year span he took part in operations throughout several hemispheres. It all began with pre-mission training for his first trip to Laos and ended with a 3-year tour in the Panama Canal Zone at Ft. Gulick with the 8th Special Forces Group (Airborne) in December 1965. During this five-year period he spent time in Nicaragua, Guatemala, Ft. Carson, Ft. Knox and Ft. Bragg, assigned as a member of the training cadre providing training for new Special Forces soldiers and Cuban Rangers for the Bay of Pigs Invasion. All in addition to the two, six-month tours in Laos. When he was not taking part in operational missions, he was undergoing branch proficiency training and medical training at Ft. Sam Houston and Ft. Bragg. This breakneck pace left little time for his family. Unfortunately, this scenario played out among many SF families and, ultimately; they could not withstand the pressures and strains of secrecy and separation placed on their personal lives.

This shortage of men in Special Forces was the impetus for expansion. This manpower shortage ensued because of the small number of trained men already deployed with teams were overtaxed. Many men who returned from Laos received orders placing them on a team slated for deployment to Vietnam or returning to Laos. Additionally, the influx of younger and inexperienced volunteers for Special Forces, undergoing the long training process, created a backlog of available trained personnel.

CHAPTER 20
LEAVING LAOS

By late 1962 the Kha program was terminated, with only twelve of the twenty-four authorized units trained. The same political decisions that brought Special Forces into contact with the tribes also removed them from Laos, often leaving the men with a feeling of abandoning their allies. "It was so sad to leave them after training them. We took them back to where they lived and cached their weapons,"[232] recalls Maggio. The feelings of bitterness and the frustration of not having clear, defined overall goals were evident with the 'here today, gone tomorrow' policies. Fred Hardy shared his perspective, "That is the same thing I think happened to the tribesmen all the way. We enticed them into coming on our side, then we pulled out—everybody—we just did not take into consideration what I think we were doing."[233] The men, who worked and lived with the people gained an understanding of them, grew close to them and felt betrayed when they had to leave their allies behind. The men of Special Forces believe fervently in their mission and the driving desire to accomplish their mission directly conflicts with events outside of their control. In spite of these feelings, the medics are quick to point out the success and feelings of pride and accomplishment. Fred Hardy said, "I think they became aware, like if they had body lice I would like to think they became aware of doing a little more washing than what they were accustomed to, but without medications or anything…"[234]

The emergence of a long-standing admiration between the Special Forces trooper and the indigenous tribes of Southeast Asia had its genesis in Laos. The simple, gentle and noble people from the tribes touched a place in all Special Forces members who served with them. How could it not, after witnessing their eagerness to learn and their countless acts of bravery? Fred Hardy relayed a story about the subtle, yet simple differences between their two worlds meeting, that aptly describes why these people are so endearing; "Some of them had never seen ice. I thought I may have a cholera epidemic on hand. I sent down for some cholera vaccine and they sent it up in a thermos jug with ice. When they saw the ice they could not believe it. They held it, rubbed it, it was the most amazing thing they had ever seen."[235]

U.S. troops were forced to leave Laos because the Geneva Agreements of June 1962 guaranteed neutrality and independence for Laos under a new government. Three political factions comprised the new government, Neutralist, Leftist and Rightist, known as Government of National Union. All three were to share the decision-making responsibilities for national defense, foreign policy and security matters. The neutrality of Laos was to be monitored and supervised by the International Control Commission (ICC). All WHITESTAR teams left the country on October 6, 1962. Angelone recalls that everyone had to be checked out of Vientiane by the ICC when WHITE STAR closed down. "They personally checked on every man on WHITE STAR teams who left in '62. That was supposed to be the end to the whole damn thing…"[236] Even though there was disgust and aggravation derived from the whole exercise, Angelone provides a summation of his feelings about the medical effort in Laos.

> "I just enjoyed being able to do something for these people. The biggest thing that shocked me, the people had no indication about the simple things, like field sanitation, purifying water, how to take care of a cut, just a small laceration. We showed them how to keep a wound clean, how to keep a clean dressing on, keep it out of the mud…I think the preventive medicine aspect was greater than the treatment. They really were starting to come around."[237]

The frustrations and difficulties of an ill-defined mission also extended to the six surgeons who participated in Laotians operations. The surgeons, at this time, did not directly command the individual medics deployed with their respective rotational deployment. Indirectly, this provided a certain degree of flexibility for each individual surgeon to develop a 'vision' based on his interests and understanding of the mission. Overall, the surgeon's priority was supporting the medics in the field. Many provided medical care for embassy staff, MAAG personnel and inevitably became a 'go between' with the multiple third country agencies and organizations supporting Laotian medical efforts. The medical officers usually had a brief service obligation to fulfill and had very little understanding of military administration. Their efforts, supporting the scattered FTT's, invariably found them attempting to coordinate and organize communications and programs among French military surgeons, Thai and Filipino medical teams, medical missionaries from multiple countries, US Public Health and State Department officials. The remoteness of teams, combined with the weather, rugged terrain and lack of air transportation, presented major obstacles for these men. To their credit, they all provided feedback from their experiences which greatly enhanced the future of SF medical development.

EPILOGUE

A DECADE OF DEDICATION

It is important to recognize that Special Forces deployed worldwide, not just in Southeast Asia, during the first decade of operations. They responded to country's requests for assistance under sensitive political climates that required an ability to project a professional manner to act as 'field ambassadors'.

The Special Forces medics' innate and extraordinary ability to leave a positive impression upon those in which he came into contact is a central theme among former team members and commanding officers. Their personal recollections and insights lend an understanding and appreciation of the team 'Doc' and his intrinsic value contributing to the successful completion of assigned missions.

Since the story began in June 1952 with the formation of the 10th Special Forces Group (Airborne), it seems providence that a mission conducted by a Special Forces Detachment of the 10th Special Forces Group (Airborne) is recounted to close out this portion of the story of the SF medic. The mission took place in Iran in 1962. Detachment A-33, 10th Special Forces Group (Airborne) received orders on 1 June 1962.

> "The primary purpose of this mission is to recover and evacuate the bodies of Lt. Col. Johnson, Maj. Carder and Capt. Knotts, presumed dead in the Zagros mountains as a result of the US Army aircraft crash on 27 January 1962...Search and recovery operations will be conducted in the simplest and most expeditious means possible. Undue risk of life for the purpose of recovering bodies or equipment is not justified. If the opera-

> tion is unsuccessful after fourteen days, you will contact this headquarters for further guidance."[238]

A letter from Colonel Herbert Y. Schandler (Ret.) dated July 27, 2000, 38 years after the mission, conveys the immense respect and deep admiration in which detachment Commanding Officers maintain for their team 'Doc' and his impact upon the mission. In his letter, Schandler relates the secondary mission of the detachment was to,

> "liaison with the native Bahktiari tribe in the region. This liaison was accomplished largely through the excellent work of my three medics, SFC Coy Melton, SFC Joseph Lisi and SSgt David A Smith. Their work with the native population was stupendous and earned us friends with the people they treated, the admiring throngs who gathered to watch them, and the chief of the tribe. SFC Melton was fluent in Pharsi, having attended the Defense Language School for 18 months. Actually, he was the only person in the village who could read and write Pharsi. SFC Lisi had been to a 100 hour Berlitz course in Munich and was fairly fluent. Both SFC Lisi and Melton had conducted classes in Pharsi for the rest of the team."[239]

His praise for the medics was unending. Schandler pointed out the fact that Sergeant First Class Melton was assigned to the team as a third medic because he was fluent in Pharsi. This conveys the vital importance of detachment members being able to converse with indigenous persons in their own language.

Initial rescue attempts by other military units resulted in rescuing two survivors. One of the deceased crew members had been located and identified but was lost during a snowstorm prior to evacuation. Severe weather conditions in the high elevation, coupled with a lack of proper equipment necessitated the search for the remaining and presumed dead, crewmembers to be suspended. Another search launched on 10 February 1962 succeeded in only recovering a minimal amount of equipment. Unexpected bad weather dropping more than a meter of snow and the inability of a HU-1B helicopter to operate at such high altitudes forced abandonment to await more favorable conditions to retrieve the remaining bodies located at 12,500 feet under 5 meters of snow. Detachment A-33 was given the opportunity to conduct the body and equipment recovery and destroy the aircraft where other elite units from Iran and Germany had failed. The teams' secondary mission was to conduct area familiarization and orientation studies.

The political sensitivity in Iran demanded the team, not receive or create publicity regarding their activities. Captain Schandler's understanding of the reason the mission was sensitive was due to a treaty that had been signed between the United States and the Soviet Union in 1945/46 that led to the removal of military units from Iran and that neither side would re-introduce such units. He felt that MAAG was sensitive to their insertion, as it may be interpreted as a "unit, thus breaching the treaty."[240] The team received specific instructions to preclude any such interpretations; "There will be no mention of Special Forces during the operation. Your personnel will wear no Special Forces insignia or berets while in Iran."[241] The Letter of Instruction received by the Detachment Commander Captain Herbert Y. Schandler, conveys the importance of Special Forces ability to conduct sensitive operations with utmost professionalism. "You and your men are direct representatives of this unit and the United States government. You will govern your actions and conduct that reflect the highest standards of discipline, appearance and professional ability."[242]

The team traveled to Kurang village in the Kurang Valley, located at the base of the mountain ridge where the crash occurred. The village is nestled in the foothills of the Zagros Mountains at the head of the Kurang Valley. The population of 400–500 Bahktiari tribe members depends on their herds of sheep, goats and donkeys to provide them a meager existence. They are Muslims, whose livelihood is also augmented by wheat farming. They are a friendly but primitive people with no outside contact with the world. A spring at the center of the village provides water that also flows down joobs lining the two streets lined with mud hut living quarters.

From here, they traveled a rough road fifteen miles into the mountains where they established a base camp on June 6. A recovery party began their ascent to the crash site and established the High Camp on June 8. The arduous journey traversed a ridge-line with sharp, abrupt cliff faces that were known to be susceptible to snow cover ranging from the 1000 foot to the 8000 elevation levels. To reach the target area required crossing a ridge-line at the 14,500 foot level and descending to the crash site at the 12,500 foot elevation. Another route through a ravine, was more direct but intelligence from MAAG indicated that it would likely no longer be passable by ski or toboggan, as the snow would probably be melted, filling the ravine with run off water. The ensuing climb to the High Camp exhausted the men, as the use of pack animals was not possible the entire distance.

In addition to the weather there were supply problems and an ecological occurrence which could not possibly have been planned for, that complicated the conduct of the mission. A natural phenomenon and an unchecked error by the team prior to their departure from Bad Tolz created a shortage in a most basic supply need—water. MAAG assured the team that there was plenty of water available on the mountain. They were apparently unaware that "All water sources at high camp are contaminated by millions of dead locust. Their live brethren make life miserable here."[243] Schandler added, "They were a nuisance. They precluded our melting snow to [be used for] drink[ing], so water had to be dropped in by air. The locust sometimes got into the food or coffee when cooking or boiling water."[244] Captain Larry A. Thorne, Executive Officer led the recovery party at the high camp and added, "Clouds of millions of locusts (grass hoppers) had descended on the area and died, contaminating snow and water supply points. In some places, dead locusts covered the ground so thickly that were walking over them like walking in deep mud."[245]

This necessitated a request for water to be dropped by parachute. The first drop was unsuccessful, due to the parachutes breaking and not opening, causing the containers to burst upon impact. A second request had to be relayed through the MAAG office in Tehran because, although communications to Bad Tolz were excellent, the team couldn't encode or decode messages on the One-Time pads. "The messages received can not be deciphered as one half of the two different sets of pads we received one complete set. Therefore, we cannot decode messages from Bad Tolz, and they cannot decode our messages."[246] Additionally, "The MAAG originally objected to this—as snow was plentiful. But, when apprised of the situation, there was no problem getting water dropped in."[247]

One of the most significant hindrances to supply operations was the failure to account and plan for cultural holidays. Muslims observe the Sabbath on Friday, which translated to both American and Iranian offices being closed. Additionally, American offices closed on Sunday's. The operation was also conducted during a Muslim religious holiday. Everything closed down on June 12 and 13. The liaison officer was frustrated by down time while trying to fulfill urgent requests for aerial re-supply. The in-country personnel should have been aware of these unique operational area circumstances—the team, however, was completely unaware of the religious aspects.

In spite of the obstacles, the mission was completed successfully several days in advance of the required time allotment. All of the bodies had been recovered, salvageable equipment secured and the aircraft was destroyed. The in-action of MAAG officials as the team departed Tehran displayed the distaste for SF prevalent in the U.S. military despite their abilities, professionalism and accomplishments. Captain Schandler's After Action Report noted "the troops involved in the rescue operation were somewhat disappointed that no one from ARMISH/MAAG Headquarters personally recognized their efforts by appearing to thank them or see them off at the airport."[248]

This mission offered valuable medical experience and intelligence. The medical conditions encountered were as would be expected in undeveloped countries. Major cities, such as, Tehran and Esfahan, lacked standard sanitation conditions. This was most noticeable in the handling of meat and the availability of potable water. Meat was completely covered with flies and showed obvious signs of decomposition. The modern hotels in the heart of the cities had potable water, which had been chemically treated and was pathogenic free. However, the other areas of the cities used water from the open gutter systems, or Joobs, for drinking, cooking, and washing clothes and dishes, watering animals and all other purposes.

A wealth of medical intelligence was gathered while conducting beneficial civic action programs for the people to encourage friendship and goodwill. It was in the village of Kurang, where the medics really displayed their abilities. Their contributions of lending aid to a population's medical needs earns the respect and admiration of not just the people they treat but that of all the team members who are well aware of the medics value to a mission.

A young graduate of the University of Tehran provided the only medical aid available for the people. He spent four months of the year in the village. Although this doctor was provided and paid by the Iranian Ministry of Public Health, the team soon learned that he charged for services, which the villagers could ill afford.

The medics' ability to incorporate the sanction of the local leadership into a treatment process for villagers is of absolute necessity. In this case, the regional tribal leader, or Khan, that went by the name Modreh Khan, "was most pleased if we would establish a dispensary for his people. He stated he would spread the word for all his people with small sicknesses to report to our camp."[249]

The medics began treating local villagers within a few days of their arrival. Captain Shchandler's report noted "The two medics in base camp, SFC [Coy] Melton and SGT [David A.] Smith, have been kept very busy in treating the local tribesmen. In gratitude and in payment, these poor people have brought in large amounts of goat milk and cheese."[250]

The dispensary was set up at a water source approximately 200 meters from the main base camp utilizing an ambulance obtained from the MAAG motor pool. Word spread quickly that limited medical help was available from the American soldiers. Patients came from as far away as two days journey by foot and donkey. The standard medical supplies for deployment SOP of 10th Group was an M-3 and M-5 kits with an additional M-5 bag packed for PROJECT MERCURY (IEP 2020) Recovery Mission.[251] Additional medical supplies were requested seven days after their first treatments of the local villagers.

Captain Schandler's report noted "The people of this region are devout Muslims and have many superstitions and non-factual beliefs and taboos. Our diagnosis was handicapped at times by this attitude. The stock answer to our question of how an injury occurred would be, 'God did it' or 'Allah gave it to me.'"[252]

The value of the medic's work and the desperate need for everything from basic medical attention to further treatment at a better equipped facility is glaringly apparent from Captain Schandler's report and from the medics daily patient log.[253]

> "During our stay we saw on the average of forty to fifty patients a day.[Authors Note: An average of 70 patients per day were treated] They would arrive as early as 0600 hours and as late as 2000 hours. The majority of the ailments were respiratory diseases, colds, bronchitis, laryngitis, strep throat, pneumonia and possible tuberculosis. Intestinal ailments were common, and approximately 90% of the people treated suffered from constipation. About 80% of the people seen, suffered from worms. Because of the absence of personal hygiene, many kinds of dermatitis were observed. A great many of the people had conjunctivitis and trachoma due to the oily type of brush they burned in their tents. The eye became irritated from the smoke and became infected. In these people we saw no evidence of venereal diseases. Birth control was discussed with some of the women at their request. A young man came to us with the problem that he was incapable of having an erection. Athletes' foot was had by the majority of the patients and many of them had severe cases that were infected. Most of the people were barefoot. One case of gas gangrene was treated."[254]

Many of the ills that afflicted the people were easily preventable. The role of educator places responsibility with the medic to provide preventive solutions to combat basic sanitation and medical problems the people of a region are experiencing. The people of Kurang lived inside their tents alongside their goats, sheep and chickens. They drank from the same water used for bathing and relieving themselves and their herds. Waste was indiscriminately disposed among their living areas. To address this problem and help the people to help themselves once the medics left, "A small training program was established and the local school teacher and some of the leading citizens of this area were given instruction in public sanitation and personal hygiene. The school teacher then repeated this instruction to his school children and, even in the short time we were present, some improvement could be seen."[255] Captain Schandler explained that, "The program was very basic…don't live with the animals, urinate downstream, etc. really basic things."[256]

Dental care was also needed. Surprisingly, even though the villagers lacked basic dental hygiene practices, their teeth were in relatively good order. Some small cavities were filled but larger ones as well as tooth extraction went untended due to the lack of proper equipment. This lack of proper equipment and more extensive training was noted in the "Lessons Learned and Recommendations" section of the final report. The medics ability to perform limited dental work can and would lend significant assistance to not only improving indigenous persons health but is an invaluable tool in winning confidence and support from the people for providing aid and relief.

The mission was a tremendous success in many respects, but as with all deployments, there were instances to learn from and improve upon to better enable future teams that could possibly deploy to the same area. Some of the significant learned lessons included;

> "Of primary importance is training in preventive medicine. The medic should be able to instruct the people in personal hygiene and sanitation and show the people how to establish their cities and tents in regard to sanitation. The medics should

also be trained to some extent in the treatment of sick animals. Many people brought their animals in for treatment."[257]

The type of mission to be conducted must also be considered and planned for with proper supplies accordingly.

> "The SOP for medical bag packing was sufficient for a guerrilla or counter-insurgency mission in a warfare zone but lacked adequate supplies for a civic action scenario. Diseases and ailments prevalent to an area commitment should receive consideration and packed accordingly. An emphasis should be placed on preventive medicines and treatment of infections. Dental equipment along with the Combat Surgical Chest should be taken. Many people were denied treatment, [such as] extractions, because of the lack of equipment."[258]

Last, but not least, an ability to speak and understand the local people's language was "Of utmost importance, it is imperative that the medic have a working knowledge of the native tongue. If he is going to be effective in treating these people."[259]

Overall, the medics had an impressive and lasting impact upon the people of the region.

> "We found these Baktiari people to be very hospitable, hard working and appreciative. Many patients sent foodstuffs to us in return for out medical efforts, food that they could ill afford to spare. We always had a crowd of interested and approving tribesmen around the aid station. We quickly made friends with these cheerful people and established a fine relationship with them. We feel that the medical care furnished these people gained us many friends. We are certain that if we were to operate in this area, we could rely on the people for 100% support. As the village chief said to us, 'These people will remember you for twenty years.'"[260]

A Letter of Commendation from the Commanding General of U.S. Forces in Europe recognized the value of the highly trained and versatile unit.

> "This demonstration is particularly significant at this stage of development of the Special Warfare concept and constitutes further justification of the confidence placed by the President in the ability of the U.S. Army Special Forces in this new role."[261]

Perhaps, the comments of the 10th Special Forces Group Surgeon best articulates the long-term benefits reaped through the medical civic action programs conducted by the medics of Detachment A-33.

> "It was apparent to this expedition that the Americans are highly regarded, and the friendly relations established among this tribe have given us the opportunity to return and be greeted as old friends. No other foreigners enjoy such prestige in this area as do the members of this Special Forces expedition. There is much work of a public health and medical nature to be done since these people lack everything. Their standard of living cannot probably be raised significantly unless they change from nomads to agricultural farm dwellers or more settled herdsmen. At present they are a large, virile, strong tribe who are well disposed towards us and who would most likely be valuable friends in time of war in this area."[262]

The successful completion of the mission also added to the prestige and justification for such a force within the U.S. Army at a time when Special Forces was under great scrutiny. A Letter of Commendation from Major Charles M. Simpson III reads, in part, "As commander of the recovery expedition you carried out a difficult mission with an absolute minimum of time, support and personnel. You succeeded where three previous attempts had failed. Your mission was accomplished with dispatch, efficiency, and no injury to the recovery personnel or loss of equipment. Your detachment contributed immeasurably to the success of your mission and demonstrated their high state of training, discipline and morale by performing additional Civic Action tasks."[263]

After a decade of dedication Special Forces stood at the threshold of a conflict that would come to be the definition of counter-insurgency warfare. The early years struggles prior to Vietnam involvement and the evolutionary triumph in the face of many obstacles and deterrents contributed and impacted the medics that served in Vietnam dramatically. Along with the successes came failures. The knowledge that came from success and failure was integrated into the training and operational use that contributed to the overall scheme and goals of the medical program, past and present.

APPENDIX 1

Standard Army Special Forces A Detachment (1963 Type)*

1 Detachment Commander, Team Leader, Captain (0-3)

1 Detachment Executive Officer, Team XO, First Lieutenant (0-2)

1 Operations Sergeant, Team Sergeant, Master Sergeant (E-8)

1 Heavy Weapons Leader, Heavy Weapons NCO, Sergeant First Class (E-7)

1 Light Weapons Leader, Light Weapons NCO, Sergeant First Class (E-7)

1 Intelligence Sergeant, Intel Sergeant, Sergeant First Class (E-7)

1 Medical Specialist, Team Medic, Specialist 7th Class or Sergeant First Class (E-7)

1 Radio Operator Supervisor, Senior Radio Operator, Sergeant First Class (E-7)

1 Assistant Medical Specialist, Junior Medic, Specialist 6th Class or Staff Sergeant (E-6)

1 Demolitions Sergeant, Engineer Sergeant, Staff Sergeant (E-6)

1 Combat Demolitions Specialist, Demo Sergeant, Specialist 5th Class or Sergeant (E-5)

1 Chief Radio Operator, Junior Radio Operator, Sergeant (E-5)

* SOURCE: Chart 1, Green Berets at War

APPENDIX 2

ORGANIZATION OF U.S. SPECIAL FORCES MEDICAL PLATOON.

MEDICAL PLATOON HEADQUARTERS

Medical operations and training officer, CPT, MSC	1
Medical supply officer, CPT, MSC	1
Chief medical NCO, E8	1
*Medical supply specialist, e5	1
*Medical records specialist, E4	1
*Clerk typist, E4	1
MEDICAL TEAM	
Dental officer, CPT, DC	1
General medical officer, CPT, MC	1
Internist, CPT, MC	1
Chief dispensary NCO, E7	1
Chief laboratory specialist, E5	1
Medical laboratory specialist, E5	1
*Pharmacy specialist	1
Senior medical aidman, E5	2
X-ray specialist, E5	1

Dental assistant, E4	1
Medical aidman, E4	3
*Medical records specialist, E4	1
PREVENTIVE MEDICINE TEAM	
Preventive medicine officer, MAJ, MC	1
Sanitary engineer, CPT, MSC	1
Veterinary officer, CPT, VC	1
Chief preventive medicine NCO, E6	1
Environmental specialist, E5	1
Food inspection specialist, E5	1
Preventive medicine specialist, E5	1
*Clerk typist, E4	1
MEDICAL OPERATIONS TEAMS (4)	
General medical officer, CPT, MC	4
Field medical assistant, LT, MSC	4
Medical operations sergeant, E7	4
Chief preventive medicine NCO, E6	4
Senior medical supply specialist, E5	4
*Medical records specialist, E4	4

*Parachute but not Special Forces qualified

Source: Medical Support of Special Warfare, Study Guide 433, US Army

Medical Field Service School, BAMC, Ft. Sam Houston, Texas, June 171, p. 9–10

APPENDIX 3

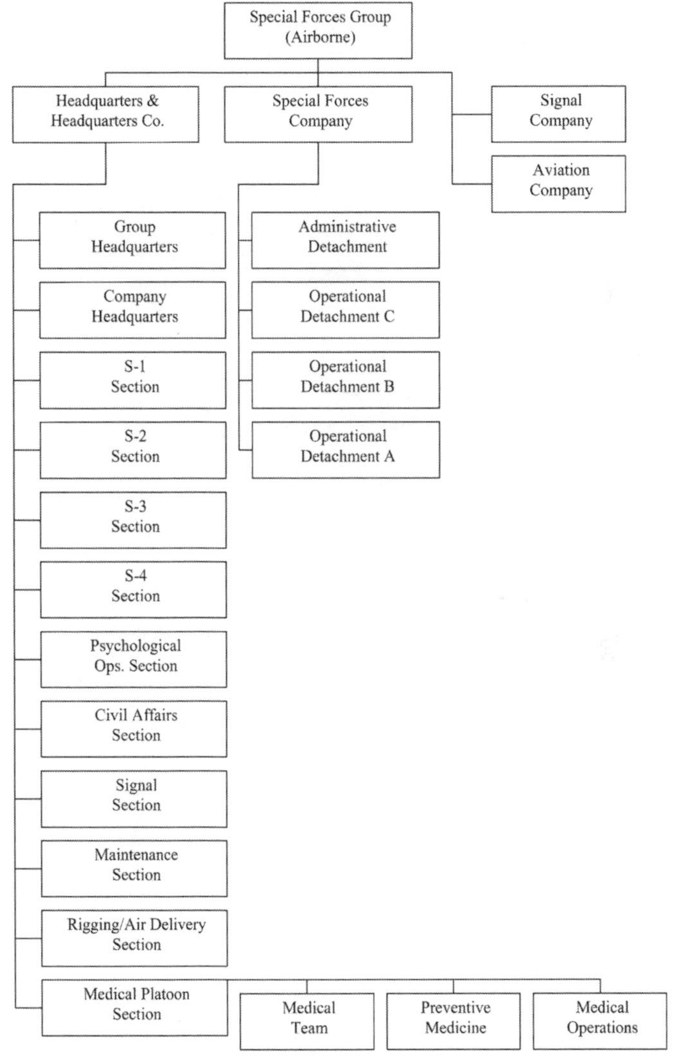

Source: Medical Support of Special Warfare, Study Guide 433
US Army Medical Field School, Brooke Army Medical Center
Fort Sam Houston, Texas, June 1971

APPENDIX 4

SERGEANT FIRST CLASS ALAN B. MAGGIO

The President of the United States of America, authorized by Act of Congress, July 2, 1926, has awarded the Soldier's Medal to

SERGEANT FIRST CLASS ALAN B. MAGGIO, USA

Sergeant First Class Maggio, a member of the 77th Special Forces Group (Airborne), distinguished himself by heroism at Fort Bragg, North Carolina, on 30 March 1954. While in his unit supply room, he heard a large crash. Running out he observed that a C-119 aircraft had crashed into a mess hall building in the area. Realizing the possibilities of an explosion, he first tried to warn personnel away from the area. With complete disregard for his own safety, he then ran into the flaming wreckage to assist in the rescue of injured personnel. He remained until all personnel had been removed and the fire was completely under control. Sergeant First Class Maggio's prompt and courageous action was instrumental in saving the lives of injured personnel and reflects great credit upon himself and the military service.

APPENDIX 5

MEDICAL DIVISION
SPECIAL FORCES OPERATIONAL SPECIALTIES DEPARTMENT
UNITED STATES ARMY INSTITUTE FOR MILITARY ASSISTANCE
Fort Bragg, North Carolina 28307

The following is a listing of the Program of Instruction of the Special Forces Basic Aidman's Course (MOS 91A):

Subject	Hours Alloted
General Subjects	14
Anatomy and Physiology	27
Common Medical Diseases	22
Pharmacology	20
Medical Techniques	30
Management of Specific Emergency Cond.	47
Nursing Techniques	54
Preventive Medicine	25
Transportation and Care of the Sick and Wounded	22
Reviews	12
Examinations	22
TOTAL	295 hours

The following is a listing of the Program of Instruction of the Special Forces Aidman's Course, MOS 91B, Fort Sam Houston, Texas:

Department and Subjects	**Hours Alloted**
Department of Dental Science	(10)
Dental First Aid	10
Department of Medicine and Surgery	(255)
Orientation Subjects	3
Basic Science Subjects	26
Pharmacology	36
Medical Conditions	64
Surgical Conditions	25
Medical and Surgical Nursing Care Procedures	74
Examinations, Discussions, and Reviews	27
Department of Military Sciences	(2)
Aeromedical Evacuation	2
Deparment of Neurophsychiatry	(9)
Basic Combat Psychiatry	9
Department of Preventive Medicine	(35)
Military Preventive Medicine	35
Department of Pathology and Laboratory Sciences	(29)
Clinical Laboratory	29
Department of Veterinary Science	(12)
Special Forces Aspects of Veterinary Preventive Medicine and Animal Care	12
Department Instructional hours (Total):	360

Following is a listing of the Program of Instruction of the Special Forces O J T Hospital Rotation and Clinical Experience section of MOS 91B Course.

Subject		Hours Alloted
Emergency Room		40
Dispensary or Outpatient Service		24
General Medicine Service		56
General Surgery Service		56
Orthopedic Service		24
Dental Service		24
Laboratory		8
Dermatology		24
Pediatrics		24
	TOTAL	280

The following is a listing of the Program of Instruction of the Special Forces Advanced Medical Training School:

Subject		Hours Alloted
Orientation		2
Patient Diagnosis		8
Human Diseases		56
Emergency Medical Treatment		20
Pediatrics		5
Psychiatry		1
Drugs		7
Anasthesia		5
Operation Room Procedures		1
Patient Care		2
Surgical Procedures		94
Pharmacy		12
Laboratory Procedures		20
Reviews		6
Examinations		16
	TOTAL	260 Hours

Source: MSG Alan B. Maggio (Ret.) Contained in author files.

APPENDIX 6

STAFF SERGEANT BILLIE A. HALL
DA General Order 18 dated
18 April 1967 (extract) II—
DISTINGUISHED SERVICE CROSS.

By direction of the president, under the provisions of the Act of Congress, approved 25 July 1963, the Distinguished Service Cross for extraordinary heroism in action, is awarded, posthumously, to: Staff Sergeant Billie A. Hall, RA18621886, United States Army. On 9 March 1966, Special Forces Detachment A-102 at Camp Ashau was subjected to a mortar barrage and small arms fire. After a day of continuous enemy bombardment, Camp A Shau was attacked by two North Vietnamese Regiments. With the advantage of surprise, superior firepower and bad weather the enemy hurled wave after wave of troops at the weakening defenses on Camp A Shau. The vicious battle forced the evacuation of the camp, and resulted in heavy casualties on both sides. Sergeant Hall, a medic, had accompanied a company of one hundred and forty-three men to reinforce Camp A Shau. When the attack started, Sergeant Hall grabbed his weapon and aid kit and ran from his quarters. Seeing many wounded in the center of the camp he ran through the enemy fire to assist in dragging the wounded to safety and treating them. Throughout the bombardment, he ran from position to position treating the wounded. Seeing two wounded Americans lying on a road in the center of the camp in the midst of numerous mortar explosions, Sergeant Hall ran to their aid. With enemy mortar rounds bursting all around him, he reached the two men and dragged them into a ditch and gave them medical aid. A direct hit on this trench killed one of the wounded Americans, an interpreter and wounded two other Americans nearby. Although Sergeant Hall had both his legs blown off when this round exploded, he refused medical attention. Being the only qualified medic at that location, he realized his responsibility to the wounded. Only after these men were treated and moved did he allow himself to be carried to the dispensary. On reaching the dispensary, though in extreme pain and weak from great loss of blood, Sergeant Hall permitted only slight treatment of his severe wounds to stem the flow of blood so he might live longer to direct operations at the aid station. Through an interpreter, he directed indigenous medics in caring for the wounded. He continued this gallant task until his body could withstand no more the demands being placed upon it, and he lapsed into a coma and died. Sergeant Hall's conspicuous gallantry and intrepidity at the cost of his own life, was a continuous inspiration to the entire garrison of Camp A Shau. His sacrifice was the spark needed to ignite the flame of desire in each man to repulse the relentless enemy as long as means were available. Sergeant Hall's unimpeachable valor in close combat was in keeping with the highest traditions of the military service and reflects great credit upon himself, his unit, and the United States Army.

APPENDIX 7

STATEMENT

7 October 1963

"I the undersigned as Detachment Sergeant of SFC Alan B. Maggio, during the period 20 March–26 September, 1962, in Laos, have personal knowledge that he was under Communist Pathet Lao small arms fire while serving in the capacity of Infantry Advisor to Kha Tribesmen.

Due to operational commitments of the detachment in the Kha program during the period 1 April–25 September 1962, it was necessary to assign SFC Maggio as Senior Infantry Advisor to Company K8, Kha Tribesmen. During this period SFC Maggio accompanied K8 on all operations and was under enemy small arms fire on numerous occasions and specifically on 20 August 1962, in the vicinity of Tayune, Laos, while accompanying a combat patrol that was ambushed by Communist Pathet Lao forces.

JAMES O. SCHMIDT
Sgt Maj (E9), Co C, 7th SFG (Abn), 1st SF
Fort Bragg, N.C.

APPENDIX 8

<u>The following letter was sent to COL Simons</u>:

THE TOM DOOLEY FOUNDATION, Inc

Ban Houei Sai, Laos, March 23, 1962

Dear Colonel Simons:

I wish to report to you the following incident which happened last night March 22, here in Ban Houei Sai.

A 35 year old Lao male was brought to me in critical condition requiring immediate surgery. I am the only doctor in an area of several hundred miles of Lao and Thai territory. Together with one American ex-Navy corpsman, by name of Al Harris, we just recently arrived in Ban Houei Sai as forerunners of a medial team belonging to the Tom Dooley Foundation. We are just starting to reorganize some basic medical facilities and without more help, with no electricity and the operating table still out of [use,] we found ourselves totally unprepared to cope with such [an] urgent and serious operation. It was at this point that we called on the local White Star team exposing our problem. The response was immediate and unanimous. Under the skilled direction of Captain Ellison we witnessed a tremendous display of how discipline and technical skill can be used with military efficiency for humanitarian purposes. In less than one hour the operation room had been set up and outfitted with electric lights. An emergency stand by power unit was just one of the many finer touches of theoretical "know how" practically applied in an urgent life-saving "do now". Each one of the six man team pitched in and the successful outcome of the operation is a tribute to the entire team, but special credit should also be given to each single individual. So for example Sergeant Murphy found himself forced in substituting for a missing anesthetist, applying to the fullest his medical training. Sergeant Rice not only procurred the electrical power, but he also improvised and operating light, while Sergeant Derringer successfully won his private struggle with the barrel and fittings of the sterilizator.

As a civilian I wish to express to, Sir, my admiration for the White Star team in Ban Houei Sai. The patient may never know what happened while he was unconscious but I wish that more people had shared my privilege in watching the events of last night.

Never before did it occur to me so strongly that regardless of war or peace, civilians and military shall always preserve the feeling of belonging to the same family of Men.

In deep appreciation,

Sincerely;

S/Carl M. Wiedernamm, M.D.

Our thanks to Flo "Penny" Murphy for bringing this letter to our attention. SGM Virgil Murphy passed away 12/20/91. NOTE: the outpost was overrun on 5/27/62 and SGTs Murphy and Loobey were missing for 3 days.

<u>This letter is an exact reproduction from RADIX PRESS "WHO'S WHO IN HOTFOOT/WHITE STAR</u>

APPENDIX 9

Special Forces Strength In Laos 1959–1961

DATES	A Detachments		B Detachments		Control Team Members	Total Auth. Strength
	Number of Teams	Members Per Team	Number of Teams	Members Per Team		
1959–1960	12	8			11	107
Spring 1961	12	11			22	154
Summer 1961	12	12			22	166
Sep-61	18	12	4	23	22	330
Oct-61	24	12	4	23	22	402

Source: Dorogi monograph Chapter 2 PP II-32.1

APPENDIX 10

IRANIAN MISSION—MEDICAL JOURNAL: 10 and 11 June, 1962

SEX	AGE	AILMENT	Rx
F	1.25	Fungus on scalp	Wash with Phisohex, Fungicidal ointment
F	1.5	Possible Bronchitis	Penicillin/Asprin
F	1.5	Possible Bronchitis	Penicillin by IV, Crytetracycline
F	1.5	Chest Cold	, rest and fluids
M	1.5	Fungus infection, scalp/body	Wash with Phisohex, saline rinse, Bacitracin ointment, IV
F	2	2nd and 3rd degree burns on hand/wrist	Wash area with Phisohex. Dry sling dressing. Chlortotracycline. Return for treatment. Wash area w/Phisohex. Procane Penicillin, dressing sling.
F	2	Possible Bronchitis	Penicillin by IV, Aspirin
M	4	Infected scalp	Wash with Phisohex, apply Benzalkonium Chloride, Basitracin and pennicillin
M	4	Burn right foot	Debridement, penicillin inject and topically, saline rinse and dressing
M	5	Chest cold	Quytatacycline, aspirin, fluids and rest
M	8	Blood poisoning	Cold bath, and referred to hospital

SEX	AGE	AILMENT	Rx
F	9	Common Cold	Aspirin, rest, fluids
M	10	Severe infection, both feet	Debridement, pennicillin inject, codeine
M	10	Severe infection, both feet	Saline soaks, debridement, penicillin, dressing
M	10	Cavaties	ASA, referred to dentist
F	11	Congenitral deformity left arm	Referred to hospital
M	11	Chest cold and infection	Chloratctacycline, Aspirin, rest and fluids
F	12	Possible Appendicitis	, APA
F	13	Chest cold	Arrytetacycline, Aspirin, fluid and rest
M	14	Malnutrition	Ascorlic acid, proper daily diet, proper daily amount of fluids
F	20	7 Mos Pregnant, swollen feet/legs	Aspirin, Multi-Vitamin, hot soak, rest/ proper diet and no salt intake
F	20	Internal growth left armpit	Referred to hospital for surgery, hot packs and aspirin for pain
M	20	Frequent nasal hemmor- age and chest congestion	Cold packs back of neck, use of facial pressure points, Chloratetacycline, referred to hospital for cauterization of superficial blood nasal vessel
M	22	Chest Congestion, headache and constipated	Cascara Sagrada, Aspirin

SEX	AGE	AILMENT	Rx
F	23	Abdominal pain/cramps/ constipation	Cascara Sagrade w/hot tea, aspirin
M	24	Ear infection, both	Wash ears with Phisohex, apply Bacitracin ointment and cotton
M	25	Fungus on hand	Wash with Phisohex, apply Fungicidal ointment
F	26	Heart Disease	Referred to hospital
M	26	Headache	Aspirin
M	30	Diarrhea	Opium, bismuth bicarbonate
F	35	Spleen Infection	Antibiotics, Aspirin
M	35	Nasal hemmor-rage, possible strep throat, emancipated	Penicillin by IV, Ascorbic Acid, proper food and liquids
M	35	Abdominal pain/cramps/ constipation	Cascara Sagrade w/hot tea, Aluminum Hydroxide gel tablets dried taken with water after bowel movement
M	35	Sprained knee	Ace bandage, aspirin, heat application
M	35	Back Ache	Heat application, aspirin
M	40	Common Cold	Aspirin/Phenzlephrine Hydrochloride Jelly
M	40	Atheletes foot	Fungicidal ointment, foot powder
M	45	Aches/Pains	Aspirin
M	45	Possible Hernia	Referred to hospital for surgery, ace bandage, hot packs and aspirin for pain
M	45	Arthritis, knee joints	ASA, heat applications, rest

SEX	AGE	AILMENT	Rx
F	50	Infection, left ankle	Wash with Phisohex, inject penicillin, clean dressing/triangle bandage with Oxytetracycline
F	50	Constipation, stomach cramps/pains	Cascara Sagrada tablets, Flunainum tablets and fluids
F	50	Chest Congestion	Antibiotics, Aspirin
F	50	Eye irritation	Tetracane alpthalmir. Aspirin
M	50	Tooth Ache	Aspirin
M	50	Cancerous infection right temple	Saline wash and soak, penicillin IV and topically, aspirin, dressing
M	50	Eye irritation	Rinse with water, apply tetracanopthatic
F	55	Aches/Pains	Aspirin, heat applications, rest
M	60	Ruemitieim	ASA, Rest
M	60	Arthritis, left shoulder	Aspirin, heat pack, rest
F	65	Ostio Arthritis	Aspirin, apply heat, rest
M	70	Ostio Arthritis	Aspirin, apply hear, rest
M	71	Ostio Arthritis	Aspirin, apply hear, rest
*	*		Approx 70 tribesmen came with common everyday aches and pains, such as headaches, minor cuts and scratches, fever blisters etc. Treatment consisted of mild analgesics, ointments, bandages, etc.
**	**		Approx 10 patients returned over the next several days to receive further treatment for extensive treatment

BIBLIOGRAPHY

VIETNAM MILITARY LORE
LEGENDS, SHADOWS AND HEROES
Master Sergeant Ray E Bows US Army (Retired)
Bows and Sons Publishing, Hanover MA
1997 by Ray Bows

INSIDE THE GREEN BERETS
The First Thirty Years
A History of the US Army Special Forces
Charles M Simpson III
Presidio Press

CHAPTER 1 INTRODUCTION
LT COL LOUIS T DOROGI (Ret)
1978 MONOGRAPH (Unpublished)

CHAPTER 2 LAOS
LT COL LOUIS T DOROGI (Ret)
1978 MONOGRAPH (Unpublished)

SPECIAL WARFARE
Winter 1990 Vol 3 No 1
EARLY SPECIAL FORCES MEDICAL TRAINING
LT COL LOUIS T DOROGI (Ret)

MSG ALAN B MAGGIO (Ret)
Unpublished notes and manuscript provided the author for use with acknowledgement to original author

US AID OPERATIONS IN LAOS
Union Calendar No 207
House Report No 546
Seventh Report by the Committee on Government Operations
June 15, 1959
United States Government Printing Office: 1959

Library of Congress, Country Studies: Research Division of the Library of Congress under the Country Studies/Area Handbook. Program sponsored by the Department of the Army. Data as of July 1994
http://memory.loc.gov

World Planet: Destination Laos: Environment
http://www.planet.com/destinations/south_east_asia/laos/environment.html

Laos, Land and People
http://www.hawaii.edu/cseas/pubs/laos/laos.html

Codename: Copperhead
My True Life Exploits as a Special Forces Soldier
Sergeant Major Joe R Garner, US Army (Retired) with Ayrum M Fine
Simon and Schuster

POW NETWORK
http://www.pownetwork.org/bios/b/b390.htm

VERITAS Magazine
October 1970

AREA HANDBOOK FOR LAOS
Department of the Army Pamphlet No. 550–58
USG Printing Office
June 1967

The Merck Manual, 12th Edition, of Diagnosis and Therapy
David N Holvey, MD
Merck, Sharpe and Dohme Research Laboratories
Division of Merck and Co., Inc.
Rahway NJ 1972

Green Berets in the Vanguard
Inside Special Forces, 1953–1963
Chalmers Archer, Jr. 2001

Special Warfare Activities Field Inspection Visit to Okinawa, Thailand Laos, Vietnam and Malaysia
Office of the Special Assistant to the Chief of Staff, U.S. Army for Special Warfare Activities Department of the Army
2 May 1962, Brigadier General William P Yarborough and Major General WB Rosson
Proposed Locations For New CIDG and BS Camps
Detachment B-7, 5th Special Forces Group Advisory Team 96
October 17, 1963

Vietnam: A History
Stanley Karnow
Penguin Books

Elite Insignia Guide: US Special Forces Shoulder and Pocket Insignia
Harry Pugh
C and D Enterprises
1993

Medical Support of Special Warfare, Study Guide 433
US Army Medical Field Service School
Brooke Army Medical Center
Ft Sam Houston TX
June 1971

Green Berets at War : U.S. Army Special Forces in Southeast Asia, 1956–1975
Shelby L. Stanton
Ballantine Books
May 1, 1999

Who's Who From 5th SFG(A) In Vietnam
TDY and HQ, USASF-V (P)
Sherman, Stephan
Radix Press, 1995

Who's Who From 1st SFG(A) In Vietnam (Part 1 and 2)
Sherman, Stephan
Radix Press, 1995

Who's Who From Hotfoot/Whitestar
Sherman, Stephan
Radix Press, 1995

Who's Who From 7th SFG(A) In Vietnam
Sherman, Stephan
Radix Press, 1995

NOTES

1. Annex B to Training Memorandum # 3
2. Campbell, Paul. Personal letter to author. August 4, 2000.
3. Periodic adjustments have resulted in a training cycle as low as 32 weeks; however, the program has hovered around 42 weeks for most of its existence, especially during the Vietnam era. The one year time span reflects current training requirements.
4. Major Himma, Einar, MC. The Medical Bulletin of the US Army, Europe. *The Medic–10th Special Forces Group (Airborne).* Volume 21. May 1964. p 150–153
5. Special Forces Aidman's Pledge, inside front cover
6. Inside the Green Berets, Forward, p. xiii
7. Appendix 3
8. Appendix 1
9. Appendix 2
10. Ballad of the Green Beret, SSG Barry Sadler
11. At the time of this event the son was assigned to the 7th Special Forces Group (Airborne) as a medic. Names withheld for operational security purposes.
12. At the time of this event U.S. forces had not yet invaded Iraq.
13. Colonel Bank, Aaron. Letter to Major Dorogi, Louis. March 24, 1976.
14. Ibid
15. Ibid.

16. Ibid.
17. Simpson, Charles. Inside the Green Berets. Presidio Press. P. 17
18. LTC Dorogi, Louis. Special Warfare. *Early Special Forces Medical Training*. Winter, 1990, Vol. 3 No. 1. P. 29
19. Major Dorogi, Louis. Interview with SGM Julius Wyngaert. February 27, 1976
20. Colonel Bank, Aaron. Letter to Major Dorogi, Louis. March 24, 1976.
21. Ibid.
22. Ibid.
23. Ibid.
24. Ibid.
25. Ibid.
26. Maggio, Alan. Unpublished manuscript in author's files. Undated.
27. LTC Dorogi, Louis. Special Warfare. *Early Special Forces Medical Training*. Winter, 1990, Vol. 3 No. 1. P. 29
28. Campbell, Paul. Personal letter to author. August 4, 2000.
29. Ibid.
30. Maggio, Alan. Unpublished manuscript in author's files. Undated.
31. Colonel Bank, Aaron. Letter to Major Dorogi, Louis. March 24, 1976.
32. Ibid
33. Ibid.
34. Major Dorogi, Lous. Interview with SGM Montgomery, Edward L. December 19, 1976.
35. Colonel Bank, Aaron. Letter to Major Dorogi, Louis. March 24, 1976.
36. Campbell, Paul. Personal letter to author. August 4, 2000.
37. Ibid.

38. Maggio, Alan. Unpublished manuscript in authors files. Undated.
39. Major Dorogi, Louis. Interview with Madison, Grant E. October 1, 1975. P 14.
40. Drumheller, Carey. Personal letter to author. August 1, 2000.
41. Major Dorogi, Louis. Interview with Colonel Juel, Roger A., MC. February 22, 1976. P 4.
42. Army Times news clipping, in authors files. Provided by Drumheller, Carey. Undated
43. Major Dorogi, Louis. Interview with Colonel Coppedge, Richard L., MC. February 22, 1976.
44. Ibid.
45. Held every rank combined from Private to Colonel in three different countries (Britain, Canada and the United States). Saw action during the first tank assault during World War I and eventually joined the US Army when World War II broke out. During the time between the two Great Wars he attended Medical School.
46. Major Dorogi, Louis. Interview with Colonel Coppedge, Richard L., MC. February 22, 1976.
47. Campbell, Paul. Personal letter to author. August 4, 2000.
48. Ibid.
49. Campbell, Paul. Personal letter to author. December 7, 2000.
50. Maggio, Alan. Unpublished manuscript in authors files. Undated.
51. Drumheller, Carey. Personal letter to author. August 1, 2000.
52. Ibid.
53. Ibid.
54. Ibid.
55. Ibid.
56. Ibid.
57. Ibid.

58. Ibid.
59. Ibid.
60. A carbuncle consists of several boils that develop close together. They expand and join together to form a larger mass, with multiple drainage points. This mass may be deeper beneath the skin surface than simple boils. They develop slowly and may be so deep they do not drain on their own. They can be caused by poor hygiene, run-down physical condition, friction from clothing or shaving, etc.
61. Drumheller, Carey. Personal letter to author. August 1, 2000.
62. Ibid.
63. Ibid.
64. Montgomery, Edward L. Interview with Major Dorogi, Louis. December 19, 1976.
65. Ibid.
66. Drumheller, Carey. Personal letter to author. August 1, 2000.
67. Ibid.
68. Drumheller, Carey. Personal letter to author. August 1, 2000.
69. Baier, Manfred. Personal letter to author. February 24, 2001.
70. Drumheller, Carey. Personal letter to author. August 1, 2000.
71. Leonpacher, Robert J. Personal letter to author. December 12, 2001.
72. Ibid.
73. Drumheller, Carey. Personal letter to author. January 15, 2001.
74. Ibid.
75. Maggio, Alan B. Unpublished manuscript in author files. Undated.
76. Drumheller, Carey. Personal letter to author. January 15, 2001.
77. Colonel Sky, Valentine B. MC. Latter to Major Dorogi, Louis. June 30, 1976.
78. Ibid.

79. Ibid.
80. Ibid.
81. Maggio, Alan B. Unpublished manuscript in author files. Undated.
82. Ibid.
83. Campbell, Paul. Personal letter to author. December 7, 2000.
84. Ibid.
85. Ibid.
86. Appendix 4: Soldier Medal Citation—Maggio
87. Chalmers Archer was also present during the rescue efforts.
88. Maggio, Alan B. Interview with author. March 15, 2001.
89. Ibid.
90. A parachute jump was required every 90 days to remain jump qualified and continue to receive extra pay for that qualification.
91. Drumheller, Carey. Personal letter to author. January 15, 2001.
92. Colonel Bue, Sigurd. MSC. Interview with Major Dorogi, Louis. November 7, 1975.
93. Ibid.
94. Ibid.
95. Colonel Sky, Valentine B. MC Letter to Major Dorogi, Louis. June 30, 1976.
96. Colonel Juel, Roger A. MC. Interview with Major Dorogi, Louis. December 17, 1976.
97. Montgomery, Edward L. Interview with Major Dorogi, Louis. December 19, 1976.
98. Ibid.
99. Colonel Sky, Valentine B. MC Letter to Major Dorogi, Louis. June 30, 1976.
100. Ibid.

101. Archer, Chalmers Jr. Interview with Major Dorogi, Louis. August 2, 1977.
102. Archer, Chalmers, Jr. *Green Berets in the Vanguard.* Naval Institute Press. 2001. P 74–75.
103. Archer, Chalmers Jr. Interview with Major Dorogi, Louis. August 2, 1977.
104. Archer, Chalmers, Jr. *Green Berets in the Vanguard.* Naval Institute Press. 2001. P 75.
105. Campbell, Paul. Personal letter to author. December 7, 2000.
106. Montgomery, Edward L. Interview with Major Dorogi, Louis. December 19, 1976.
107. Ibid.
108. Ibid.
109. Ibid.
110. Drouin, Ralph C. Interview with Major Dorogi, Louis. October 5, 1975.
111. Major Dorogi, Louis. Unpublished manuscript. 1978.
112. Drouin, Ralph C. Interview with Major Dorogi, Louis. October 5, 1975.
113. Madison, Grant, E. Interview tih Major Dorogi, Louis. October 1, 1975.
114. Ibid.
115. Appendix 5: Program of Instruction
116. Maggio, Ala B. Unpublished manuscript in author files. Undated.
117. Ibid.
118. Ibid.
119. Maggio, Alan B. Interview with author. October 27, 2001.
120. Madison, Grant E. Interview with Major Dorogi, Louis. October 1, 1975.

121. Appendx 6: SSG Billy Hall. Distinguished Service Cross.
122. *Special Forces Operational Specialties Department;* provided by Maggio, Alan B. September 25, 1959
123. Appendix 5: Program of Instruction.
124. *Special Forces Operational Specialties Department;* provided by Maggio, Alan B. September 25, 1959
125. Dr. Skemp, Samuel. Interview with Major Dorogi, Louis. June 21, 1977.
126. Major Dorogi, Louis. Unpublished manuscript. 1978
127. Dr. Skemp, Samuel. Interview with Major Dorogi, Louis. June 21, 1977.
128. Major Dorogi, Louis. Unpublished manuscript. Laos. 1978.
129. A doctor from Thailand working independently in the region.
130. Angelone, Patsy, Interview with Major Dorogi, Louis, November 7, 1975.
131. Miller, Ned L., Interview with author, October 18, 2000.
132. Ibid.
133. Major Dorogi, Louis. Unpublished manuscript. Laos. 1978.
134. Miller, Ned L., Interview with author, October 18, 2000.
135. Also known as the Pentalateral Treaty involving France, Laos, Vietnam and Cambodia.
136. According to the Angency for International Development, U.S. aid in 1958 was listed as 36.9 million dollars.
137. Named for Brigadier General John A. Heintges who was the Chief PEO in 1958 when he began his assessment of Laotian military needs.
138. Major Dorogi, Louis. Unpublished manuscript. Laos. 1978.
139. Miller, Ned L., Interview with author, June 16, 2000.

140. Wyngaert, Julius. Interview with Major Dorogi, Louis. February 27, 1976.
141. http://www.pownetwork.org/bios/b/b390.htm
142. Dougan, Don. Interview with author. March 18, 2001.
143. Maggio, Alan B. Interview with author. March 15, 2001.
144. Appendix 7
145. Major Dorogi, Louis. Unpublished manuscript. Laos. 1978.
146. Angelone, Patsy. Interview with Major Dorogi, Louis. November 7, 1975
147. Ibid.
148. Ibid.
149. Major Dorogi, Louis. Unpublished manuscript. Laos. 1978.
150. Miller, Ned L., Interview with author, June 16, 2000.
151. Hardy, Fred. Interview with Major Dorogi, Louis. Undated.
152. Peckham, Earle K. Interview with author. June 17, 2001.
153. Miller, Ned L., Interview with author, June 16, 2000.
154. Peckham, Earle K. Interview with author. June 17, 2001.
155. Miller, Ned L., Interview with author, June 16, 2000.
156. Wyngaert, Julius. Interview with Major Dorogi, Louis. February 27, 1976.
157. Ibid.
158. Ibid.
159. Ibid.
160. Major Dorogi, Louis. Unpublished manuscript. Laos. 1978.
161. Ibid.
162. Miller, Ned L., Interview with author, June 16, 2000.
163. Miller, Ned L., Interview with author, June 16, 2000.

164. The remaining 50 were split among the other detachments operating out of Ban Huoei Sai, FTT-2 and FTT-2-A
165. Miller, Ned L., Interview with author, June 16, 2000.
166. Appendix 8: Letter from the Tom Dooley Foundation. Details concerning FTT-2, these men had taken part in a humanitarian effort prior to this incident.
167. Miller, Ned L., Interview with author, June 16, 2000.
168. Ibid.
169. Ibid.
170. Major Dorogi, Louis. Unpublished manuscript. Laos. 1978.
171. Wyngaert, Julius. Interview with Major Dorogi, Louis. February 27, 1976.
172. Ibid.
173. Ibid.
174. Major Dorogi, Louis. Unpublished manuscript. Laos. 1978.
175. Ibid.
176. Angelone, Patsy. Interview with Major Dorogi, Louis. November 7, 1975
177. Major Dorogi, Louis. Unpublished manuscript. Laos. 1978.
178. Ibid.
179. Angelone, Patsy. Interview with Major Dorogi, Louis. November 7, 1975
180. Major Dorogi, Louis. Unpublished manuscript. Laos. 1978.
181. Angelone, Patsy. Interview with Major Dorogi, Louis. November 7, 1975
182. Ibid.
183. Ibid.
184. Ibid.
185. Major Dorogi, Louis. Unpublished manuscript. Laos. 1978.

186. Angelone, Patsy. Interview with Major Dorogi, Louis. November 7, 1975

187. Miller, Ned L., Interview with author, June 16, 2000.

188. Ibid.

189. Ibid.

190. Ibid.

191. Hardy, Fred. Interview with Major Dorogi, Louis. Undated.

192. Major Dorogi, Louis. Unpublished manuscript. Laos. 1978.

193. Hardy, Fred. Interview with Major Dorogi, Louis. Undated.

194. Ibid.

195. Ibid.

196. Ibid.

197. Wyngaert, Julius. Interview with Major Dorogi, Louis. February 27, 1976.

198. Ibid.

199. Ibid.

200. Angelone, Patsy. Interview with Major Dorogi, Louis. November 7, 1975

201. Ibid.

202. Sergeant Major Garner, Joe R. with Fine, Ayrum M. *Codename: Copperhead My True Life Exploits as a Special Forces Soldier.* Simon and Schuster. P 63

203. Ibid. p 65

204. Ibid. P 65

205. Ibid. p 65

206. Ibid. p 65

207. Hardy, Fred. Interview with Major Dorogi, Louis. Undated.

208. Ibid.

209. Major Dorogi, Louis. Unpublished manuscript. Laos. 1978.
210. Miller, Ned L., Interview with author, June 16, 2000.
211. Ibid.
212. Angelone, Patsy. Interview with Major Dorogi, Louis. November 7, 1975
213. Ibid.
214. Angelone, Patsy. Interview with Major Dorogi, Louis. November 7, 1975
215. Major Dorogi, Louis. Unpublished manuscript. Laos. 1978.
216. Miller, Ned L., Interview with author, June 16, 2000.
217. Angelone, Patsy. Interview with Major Dorogi, Louis. November 7, 1975
218. Ibid.
219. Ibid.
220. Ibid.
221. US Printing Office. *Area Handbook for Laos.* Department of the Army Pamphlet No 550–58. June 1967.
222. Major Dorogi, Louis. Unpublished manuscript. Laos. 1978.
223. Ibid.
224. Radcliffe, William B. Letter to Major Dorogi, Louis. Undated.
225. Angelone, Patsy. Interview with Major Dorogi, Louis. November 7, 1975
226. Gunn, Al. Interview with author. Undated
227. Miller, Ned L., Interview with author, June 16, 2000.
228. Dougan, Don, Interview with author, March 18, 2001
229. Dougan, Don. Interview with author. March 18, 2001.
230. Appendix 9. Special Forces Strength in Laos 1959 to 1961
231. Miller, Ned L. Interview with author. October 18, 2000.

232. Maggio, Alan B. Interview with author March 15, 2001.
233. Hardy, Fred. Interview with Major Dorogi, Louis. Undated.
234. Ibid.
235. Hardy, Fred. Interview with Major Dorogi, Louis. Undated.
236. Angelone, Patsy. Interview with Major Dorogi, Louis. November 7, 1975
237. Ibid.
238. Headquarters 10th Special Forces Group (Airborne), 1st Special Forces. *Letter of Instruction.* June 1, 1962
239. Colonel Schandler, Herbert Y, Ph.D., Letter to author. July 27, 2000
240. Colonel Schandler, Herbert Y, Ph.D., Letter to author. March 26, 2003
241. Headquarters 10th Special Forces Group (Airborne), 1st Special Forces. *Letter of Instruction.* June 1, 1962
242. Ibid.
243. Captain Schandler, Herbert Y. Company C 10th Special Forces Group (Airborne), 1st Special Forces. *After Action Report: Recovery Mission to Iran, Annex B: Diary of Activities at Base Camp.* July 5, 1962.
244. Colonel Schandler, Herbert Y, Ph.D., Letter to author. March 26, 2003
245. Captain Schandler, Herbert Y. Company C 10th Special Forces Group (Airborne), 1st Special Forces. *After Action Report: Recovery Mission to Iran, Annex C: Diary of Activities at High Camp.* July 5, 1962
246. Captain Schandler, Herbert Y. Company C 10th Special Forces Group (Airborne), 1st Special Forces. *After Action Report: Recovery Mission to Iran, Annex B: Diary of Activities at Base Camp.* July 5, 1962.

247. Colonel Schandler, Herbert Y, Ph.D., Letter to author. March 26, 2003

248. Captain Schandler, Herbert Y. Company C 10th Special Forces Group (Airborne), 1st Special Forces. *After Action Report: Recovery Mission to Iran.* July 5, 1962

249. Captain Schandler, Herbert Y. Company C 10th Special Forces Group (Airborne), 1st Special Forces. *After Action Report: Recovery Mission to Iran, Annex B: Diary of Activities at Base Camp.* July 5, 1962.

250. Ibid.

251. Special Forces deployed across the globe as alternative rescue stations in case the Project MERCURY shot came down in the wrong place. The 10th Group deployed two medic diver/paratroopers in Ben Guerir, Morocco, Kano, Nigeria, Salisbury, Nairobi and other locations. (Colonel Schandler, Herbert Y. Letter to author. March 26, 2003)

252. Captain Schandler, Herbert Y. Company C 10th Special Forces Group (Airborne), 1st Special Forces. *After Action Report: Recovery Mission to Iran, Annex D: Civic Action and Medical Report.* July 5, 1962

253. Appendix 10: Iranian Mission Patient Log. Captain Schandler, Herbert Y. Company C 10th Special Forces Group (Airborne), 1st Special Forces. *After Action Report: Recovery Mission to Iran, Annex D: Civic Action and Medical Report.* July 5, 1962

254. Captain Schandler, Herbert Y. Company C 10th Special Forces Group (Airborne), 1st Special Forces. *After Action Report: Recovery Mission to Iran, Annex D: Civic Action and Medical Report.* July 5, 1962

255. Ibid. Section B

256. Colonel Schandler, Herbert Y, Ph.D., Letter to author. March 26, 2003

257. Captain Schandler, Herbert Y. Company C 10th Special Forces Group (Airborne), 1st Special Forces. *After Action Report: Recovery Mission to Iran, Annex D: Section B. Civic Action and Medical Report.* July 5, 1962

258. Ibid. Section B

259. Ibid. Section D

260. Ibid. Annex D, Part 10

261. Headquarters, United States Army, Europe, Office of the Commander in Chief. *Letter of Commendation.* July 30, 1962

262. Captain Schandler, Herbert Y. Company C 10th Special Forces Group (Airborne), 1st Special Forces. *After Action Report: Recovery Mission to Iran, Annex D: Annex D, Comments Section 2. Civic Action and Medical Report.* July 5, 1962

263. Company C, 10th Special Forces Group (Airborne), 1st Special Forces. *Letter of Commendation.* August 22, 1962

978-0-595-40256-4
0-595-40256-9

Made in the USA
Lexington, KY
03 December 2009